Lulu
the Lifeguard
Fairy

To all water babies

Special thanks to
Rachel Elliot

ORCHARD BOOKS

First published in Great Britain in 2015 by Orchard Books
This edition published in 2016 by The Watts Publishing Group

3 5 7 9 10 8 6 4 2

© 2016 Rainbow Magic Limited.
© 2016 HIT Entertainment Limited.
Illustrations © 2015 The Watts Publishing Group Ltd

HIT entertainment

The moral rights of the author and illustrator have been asserted.

A CIP catalogue record for this book is available from the British Library.

ISBN 978 1 40834 890 1

Printed in Great Britain

MIX
Paper from
responsible sources
FSC® C104740
FSC
www.fsc.org

The paper and board used in this book are made from wood from responsible sources

Orchard Books
An imprint of Hachette Children's Group
Part of The Watts Publishing Group Limited
Carmelite House, 50 Victoria Embankment, London EC4Y 0DZ

An Hachette UK Company
www.hachette.co.uk
www.hachettechildrens.co.uk

Lulu
the Lifeguard
Fairy

by Daisy Meadows

ORCHARD

www.rainbowmagic.co.uk

The Fairyland Palace

Seeing Pool

Tippington Hall

Rachel's House

Tippington Town

Jack Frost's Spell

These silly helpful folk I see
Don't know they could be helping me.
But they will fail and I will smirk,
And let the goblins do the work.

I'll show this town I've got some nerve
And claim rewards that I deserve.
The prize on offer will be mine
And I will see the trophy shine!

Contents

Teacher in Trouble

"Finally, I would like to thank my wonderful patients, who have been kind enough to nominate me for this award," said Aunt Lesley. "I look forward to continuing to help them."

On the sofa in the Walkers' sitting room, Kirsty Tate and Rachel Walker clapped with enthusiasm. Kirsty was

visiting her best friend for the spring
half term, and Rachel's Aunt Lesley was
staying there too. She was a respected
local doctor, and the girls had really
enjoyed spending time with her during
the holiday.

"Do you think that
sounds all right,
girls?" asked Aunt
Lesley, looking
nervous. "I feel a
bit silly practising
what I'll say if I
win the award."

Aunt Lesley had been
nominated for the Tippington Helper
of the Year Award. It was a local prize
that rewarded the special people in the
community who had a job helping

others, and the ceremony was that
evening at Tippington Town Hall.

"You definitely need to have a speech
ready," said Rachel. "You're bound to
win!"

"I'm not so sure," said Aunt Lesley with
a laugh. "You've met most of
the other nominees. They're
all brilliant at their
jobs."

Kirsty and Rachel
nodded.

"Isobel the firefighter
and Colin the paramedic
are wonderful," said
Rachel.

"And I'm sure Mark the lifeguard is
amazing," Kirsty added. "But we want
you to win!"

Aunt Lesley smiled at them.

"I'm so pleased that I've had your company this week," she said. "You two always seem to be having fun."

Just then, they heard the doorbell ring.

"That must be Bailey," said Rachel, jumping up. "Sorry, Aunt Lesley, but we have to go now. Bailey's mum is taking us all to the local pool."

Bailey was the boy who lived next door. The girls had helped to rescue his kitten, Pushkin, a few days earlier, and his mum was taking them to a swimming lesson as a way of saying thank you. Rachel and Kirsty said goodbye to Aunt Lesley and scooped up their swimming bags as they headed for the door. When they opened it, Bailey

was standing
there with a
big smile on
his face.

"Ready
for our
lesson?" he
asked.

"We can't
wait," said
Kirsty. "Let's go!"

They had a fun ride in
Bailey's mum's car, singing along to
the radio at the tops of their voices.
They arrived at the leisure centre and
dashed to the changing rooms to get
into their swimsuits. Then they went to
join the other children at the shallow
end of the pool.

"Isn't it brilliant that Mark's been nominated for the Tippington Helper of the Year Award?" said a blonde-haired girl in a red swimsuit. "He's such a great swimming teacher – I really think he deserves to win."

"I thought he worked as a lifeguard," said Rachel.

"He takes our lessons too," said the girl with a smile. "He thinks it's really important to learn how to swim."

"He told me that he's seen lots of people who can't swim well get into trouble in the water," said a boy in blue trunks. "Working as a lifeguard was what made him want to learn to teach swimming."

"He sounds great," said Kirsty with a big smile. "I can't wait for the lesson to start!"

Just then, a man wearing red swimming shorts came striding down the poolside towards them. He had a yellow whistle around his neck and grinned at the waiting children.

"OK, everyone, I hope you're feeling energetic!" he said in a booming voice.

"Today I'm going to show you how to do the front crawl. For this stroke you have to think about kicking, paddling and breathing all at the same time. Watch me first and then jump into the pool and we'll all try it together."

He jumped into the shallow end of the pool, but instead of starting to swim, he just thrashed about. Spluttering and shaking, he lurched towards the ladder and hauled himself out of the pool.

"Was that a new stroke?" asked Bailey. "I've never seen it before."

Rachel and Kirsty exchanged a worried glance, and Mark looked embarrassed.

"That wasn't a swimming stroke at all," he said, panting. "I've forgotten how to swim!"

Lulu Arrives

"I'm so sorry," Mark told the class. "I don't understand what just happened, but I can't take a swimming lesson if I don't trust myself in the water. I'm going to have to cancel the lesson and close the pool. There are no other lifeguards available to take over from me."

Looking very disappointed, the other children in the class wandered over to the bench to collect their towels. Rachel and Kirsty paused and watched Mark sit down on the poolside and put his head in his hands.

"Poor Mark," said Rachel. "What on earth could have made him forget how to swim?"

The others were already walking into the changing rooms. As the girls went to pick up their towels, Kirsty drew in her breath sharply.

"Look at your towel," she exclaimed. "It's glowing!"

"It's magic," said Rachel, and the best friends shared a happy smile.

Even though they had been on many magical adventures, they always felt a thrill of excitement when they had a visit from a fairy. Rachel picked up her towel and saw Lulu the Lifeguard Fairy sitting cross-legged on the bench.

"Hello, Lulu!" said Rachel. "What are you doing here?"

The little fairy jumped up, fluttering her wings. She was wearing a yellow T-shirt tied up at the front into a knot, a pair of red shorts and pink trainers that matched her whistle.

"I've come to ask for your help," she said, shaking back her shiny brown hair. "I have to find a way to get my magical rescue float back from Jack Frost and his goblins."

On the first day of Kirsty's visit to
Tippington, Martha the Doctor Fairy
had whisked the girls to Fairyland to
meet the other Helping Fairies. Jack
Frost had stolen their magical objects,
and without them the fairies couldn't
help everyday heroes
like Aunt Lesley
do their jobs.

"We'll do
whatever
you need
us to do,"
said Rachel.
"We've helped
Martha, Ariana
and Perrie to get their
magical objects back – and we'll find
yours too."

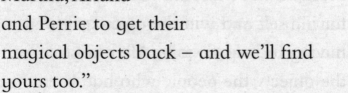

"Thank you,"
said Lulu, with
a flash of a
smile. "Jack
Frost only
has one
magical
object left,
but he's still
trying to win the
Tippington Helper
of the Year Award and he's still causing
trouble."

Jack Frost had ordered his goblins to
do the jobs of the award nominees. He
thought that he could take the credit
for himself and win the award without
having to help anyone. After he stole
the objects, the people who had been

nominated for the award had started behaving very strangely. Isobel the firefighter had stopped being brave, Colin the paramedic had panicked at the sight of a grazed knee and even Aunt Lesley had stopped helping her patients.

So far the girls had managed to get back three of the Helping Fairies' magical objects, and three of the everyday heroes were doing their jobs again and helping others. But Lulu the Lifeguard Fairy was still missing her magical rescue float.

"What sort of trouble is Jack Frost causing?" Kirsty asked.

"All lifeguards everywhere are forgetting how to swim," said Lulu. "They won't be able to help people until the float is back where it belongs."

"Mark, the lifeguard here, has forgotten how to swim too!" said Rachel. "He couldn't understand why – I think he's really upset."

They glanced over to where Mark was still sitting with his head in his hands. Luckily he wasn't paying any attention to the girls, and he hadn't spotted the little fairy perching on the bench.

"It's all because of Jack Frost," Lulu said. "Unless I find my magical rescue float, Mark will never work as a lifeguard again."

"We need to start searching for the float," said Kirsty. "Where shall we start?"

Just then they heard chatter coming from the changing rooms. Mark heard it too – he stood up and cleared his throat.

Lulu darted into Kirsty's swimming bag
as he glanced across at them.

"You'd better go and get changed,
girls," he said. "I'm afraid there will be no
lesson today."

He gave them a sad smile and strode
out of the swimming pool area.

Goblin Island

The girls headed towards the changing room, but just as they went in, Rachel stopped and tilted her head to the side.

"Do you hear something?" she asked. "There's a noise coming from the swimming pool."

Kirsty and Lulu listened too. They heard a faint splashing sound, and a few high-pitched giggles.

"Come on!" Kirsty exclaimed.

They rushed back to the pool and saw three goblins pushing a giant inflatable island into the middle of the water. They were wearing bright green swim trunks, swimming caps and goggles.

"Those naughty goblins!" said Rachel. "We should have guessed they'd be here, trying to do Mark's job."

"They don't look very interested in being lifeguards," said Kirsty.

The goblins were having a wonderful time playing on the inflatable island. It had a soft slide and a hollow to crawl through, painted like a log. Squealing and squawking, they bounced, slid, splashed and skidded around the island.

"At least one of the goblins looks
as if he wants to be a lifeguard," said
Rachel.

She pointed at a fourth goblin who
was busily swimming laps in the pool.
Just then, one of the playing goblins slid
off into the path of the one who was
swimming laps. He lifted his head out of
the water.

"Get out of my way, you green
nincompoop!" he screeched.

"Oh my goodness, that's
not a goblin!" Kirsty
said with a gasp.
"That's Jack Frost!"

His long beard
was dripping with
water and had lost
all its spikiness.

His hair was slicked back with water.

"I didn't know he was such a good swimmer," said Lulu, poking her head out of Kirsty's swimming bag.

"He's not," Rachel replied with a puzzled frown. "It wasn't very long ago that he was taking swimming lessons from the Little Mermaid at the Tiptop Castle Fairytale Festival. He can't possibly have become an amazing swimmer since then."

The girls moved closer to the pool, and Lulu let out a cry of surprise.

"He's not an amazing swimmer, he's an amazing cheater," she said. "He's using my magical rescue float to help him swim!"

Rachel and Kirsty shared an excited glance. They had found it!

"Now all we have to do is get it back for Lulu," said Kirsty. "Any ideas?"

"I've got one," said Rachel. "But we're going to have to pretend to be goblins!"

Kirsty grinned.

"We've done it before," she said. "And if it helps Lulu, I'm ready."

The girls slipped back into the corridor that led to the changing rooms. Then Lulu fluttered out of the bag and hovered in front of them.

"Are you sure about this?" she asked. "You really want me to turn you into goblins?"

"Definitely," said Rachel with a twinkle in her eyes. "As long as you turn us back again afterwards!"

Lulu laughed and raised her wand as she spoke the words of a spell.

34

"Make these girls look green and grim, ready for a goblin swim!"

Rachel and Kirsty felt their skin prickling as it grew rough and knobbly. Their hair disappeared, and their noses and ears grew bigger. In green swimsuits, goggles and swimming caps, they looked the

same as the goblins frolicking on the inflatable island.

"It's strange
to have such
big feet!"
squawked
Rachel, and
then put
her hand to
her throat.
"Ooh, I'd
forgotten that
I would sound
like a goblin too!"

Kirsty tried to laugh,
but it came out as a high-pitched goblin
giggle.

"What do you think we should do
next?" she asked.

"We need to get out to the island,"
said Rachel. "If Jack Frost thinks we're

just ordinary goblins, he won't be expecting us to try to rescue the float. Let's play with the other goblins for a while so he doesn't suspect anything. Then we'll try to grab the float."

"I'll stay close to you," Lulu promised.

"Don't let them see you," Rachel urged her.

Lulu smiled and fluttered high into the air. While the goblins were splashing around the island, she perched among the leaves of an inflatable palm tree. Kirsty took a deep breath.

"Are you nervous?" Rachel asked her.

Kirsty smiled at her best friend.

"A bit," she said. "I've pretended to be a goblin before, but never in the middle of a swimming pool!"

"We'll be fine," said Rachel, squeezing her hand. "After all, we'll be together and we're best friends. We can do anything!"

Chasing the Float

The girls ran out to the pool and dived into the water, then swam towards the island. As they pulled themselves up, dripping wet, the other goblins glared at them.

"There's not enough room on here for two more," he snapped. "Go away."

"You can't boss
us about," said
Rachel,
remembering
that she
needed to
sound as rude
as the goblins
if she was going
to fit in. "We'll do
what we want."

The other goblins grumbled under
their breath, but they didn't stop Rachel
from climbing onto the soft slide. Kirsty
crawled through the soft log, and the
other goblins didn't pay them any more
attention.

Meanwhile, Jack Frost was still
swimming laps up and down the pool.

As he came up to the side of the island, Rachel stood on top of the slide and dived into the water in front of him.

"I've told you before, you idiot!" Jack Frost bellowed angrily, treading water with the float round his middle. "Get out of my way!"

At that moment, Kirsty jumped into the water behind him. He turned and frowned at her.

"Give me that float!" said Kirsty.

"Have you both gone mad?" Jack
Frost demanded. "You can't order *me*
around!"

Rachel lunged for the float, but he
turned and splashed her in the face.
Spluttering and
coughing,
Rachel
thrashed
around in
the water
and grabbed
the side of
the island to
steady herself. Then
Kirsty grabbed at the float.

"Oh no you don't!" Jack Frost yelled as
her fingertips touched it.

He splashed water in her eyes, and
by the time she could see again he was
already halfway across the pool. She and
Rachel struck out to follow him, but he
quickly reached the ladder
and climbed out of the
pool. Shaking water
from his beard, he
tucked the float
under his arm and
glared at them.

"I'm going
home to the
Ice Castle," he
shouted, his voice
echoing around the pool
room. "I'm going to have a swim in my
own private moat, and you stupid goblins
are *not* invited!"

Jack Frost pulled his wand from a
pocket in his ice-blue swimming trunks.
He waved it, and there was a bright-blue
flash and a loud bang. Then suddenly he
had disappeared, and Rachel and Kirsty
were left treading water.

"What can we do now?" Kirsty
groaned.

"Follow him, of course!" said Lulu from
above them.

She waved her
wand, and Rachel
and Kirsty rose
out of the water,
twirling as they
transformed from
goblins into tiny
fairies, now back
in their clothes.

The goblins on the inflatable island gave
shouts of fury.

"Tricksy fairies!"

"Catch them!"

But as the goblins belly-flopped into the
water, Lulu whisked herself and the girls
to Fairyland. Still breathless from their
swim, they found themselves fluttering
above the Ice Castle moat. They could
see that Jack Frost had broken the ice to
be able to get into the water, and now he
was swimming around the moat at top
speed. Several goblins were standing on
the edge of the moat, watching him and
clapping each time he passed.

"I'm faster than a fish!" he shouted to
them. "Faster than a dolphin! No one
and nothing could be a better swimmer
than me!"

Kirsty gave a little gasp.

"I've got an idea," she said. "Oh, I hope this works! Lulu, could you magic up a special swimming trophy – something big and gaudy?"

Lulu smiled and waved her wand. Suddenly a pedestal appeared on the edge of the moat. On top of it stood a large golden cup, studded with sparkling jewels. The goblins noticed it at once, and their mouths dropped open.

"What's that?" one of them cried, darting towards it.

"I want it!" said another.

"I saw it first," said a third goblin.

"It doesn't belong to you," said Kirsty, fluttering down and perching next to the trophy. "It belongs to the winner of the swimming race."

Lulu waved her wand again, and
suddenly the edges of the moat were
decorated with banners, and a large
'Finish' sign hung above the moat near
to the fairies.

"I'm entering the race!" exclaimed one of the goblins.

"Me too!" several of the others cried out.

They pressed around the trophy, examining it so closely that

their noses brushed against it. Jack Frost climbed out of the moat and came to gaze at the beautiful trophy. He was still clutching the float tightly to his chest.

"What swimming race?" he demanded.

Rachel smiled.

"We're organising a competition to try to win the trophy," she said. "Would you like to enter?"

"Of course I'm entering!" Jack Frost shouted. "What a stupid question!"

The Great
Moat Race

"There's just one condition," said Kirsty. "To make the race fair, you can't use the float."

"Rubbish," said Jack Frost, his hands clenching around the float. "My moat, my rules."

"Yes, but it's our trophy," said Rachel. "And we say that you can't enter with a float. What do the other competitors think?"

All the goblins who wanted to join the race began to nod and complain at the tops of their voices.

"It's not fair!"

"No floats allowed!"

Jack Frost tried to argue, but the fairies shook their heads and the goblins stuck their fingers in their ears. The trophy glinted in a ray of sunlight, and Jack Frost stared at it.

"I want that trophy," he grumbled. "I've got just the right place for it in my Throne Room."

"It's up to you," said Kirsty. "If you think you can't win the race without the float, maybe you shouldn't enter."

"I don't need a silly old float to win!"

Jack Frost erupted. "I can beat the lot of you, with or without the float. I'm the amazing Jack Frost, and I will win, no matter what!"

He looked around and held out the float to the nearest goblin.

"Here, hold this," he ordered. "Look after it while I show the lot of you what a fantastic swimmer I am."

"Now, Lulu!" Kirsty whispered.

As soon as the goblin had taken the float, the Lifeguard Fairy darted forward and knocked it out of his hands. When

she touched it, the
float immediately
shrank to fairy
size. She caught
it and zoomed up
out of reach.

"Hey—" Jack Frost
started to shout, but
Lulu didn't give him the
chance to finish.

"Everyone who wants to join in
the race, on your marks," she said,
raising her whistle to her lips. "Ready,
steady…"

She gave a long, shrill blow on the
whistle and all the goblins jumped into
the moat. There was a lot of squealing
and splashing as they got used to the
freezing water.

"Wait!" Jack yelled. "I wasn't ready!"

He plunged back into the moat, while enormous goblin feet kicked and splashed icy water in his face. Panicking, he flailed about in the water, waving his arms and taking in great mouthfuls of water as he shouted.

"Help! Help!" he bellowed. "Get me out of here! I don't like it any more!"

Without the magical rescue float, he couldn't swim a single stroke. Lulu tucked the float under her arm and dived into the water. She put her arms around Jack Frost and spoke quietly in his ear, calming him down and asking him to lie flat. Then she drew him carefully back to the shallow water.

"You really should learn to swim before you go into deep water," she told him. "You could have been in real trouble then."

Jack Frost coughed up some more moat water and muttered something under his breath.

"Let Lulu help you," said Rachel. "Swimming can be fun as well as being important, you know."

Lulu asked Jack to hold on to the edge of the moat and kick his legs. When he had got the hang of that, she showed him how to paddle his arms through the water to help him to stay afloat.

"You see, you don't need my magical

float to be a good swimmer," she said
in a kind voice. "Just keep practising
and you'll soon get the hang of it. I can
see you'll make a very good swimmer
one day."

"The job of a lifeguard is very
important," said Rachel. "Don't you
think so?"

Jack Frost cleared his throat and
nodded, looking a bit embarrassed.

"I suppose it was … er … probably
quite a good thing that she was here," he
said, jerking his thumb at Lulu.

The fairies shared a smile, and then
heard a loud cheer from the spectator
goblins. Someone had crossed the finish
line. Kirsty picked up the trophy and
presented it to the dripping-wet goblin as
he clambered out of the moat.

"I hereby declare that you are the winner of the Great Moat Race!" she announced.

Everyone burst into applause – everyone, that is, except Jack Frost. He glowered at the winning goblin. But Kirsty whispered to Lulu, and she waved her wand. A scroll of paper appeared in Jack Frost's hands, and he opened it. A huge smile spread across his face.

Swimming Certificate
Awarded to Jack Frost
Swimming Champion of the Future

"It's time for us to go," said Lulu.
Among the cheers of the goblins, she
gave her wand a little flick, and the girls
were caught up in a swirl of rainbow
colours. When they could see clearly
again, they found that they were in the
Throne Room at the Fairyland Palace.

A Splendid
Ceremony

Rachel and Kirsty heard the sound of enthusiastic clapping, and then realised that the four Helping Fairies were standing in the Throne Room beside Queen Titania and King Oberon.

"You've done it!" cried Perrie, jumping up and down in excitement.

Ariana and Lulu were smiling from
ear to ear, and Martha threw her arms
around the girls and hugged them.
Queen Titania and King Oberon were
smiling too.

"Thank you from the bottom of
our hearts for all the help you give to
Fairyland," said King Oberon. "We have
something special that we would like to
give you."

Queen Titania stepped forward and
handed a little badge to each of the girls.
The picture on each badge showed two
hands clasped together.

"I hope that these
will remind
you of our
gratitude,"
said the
fairy
queen.
"You are
both always
ready to lend
us a helping
hand whenever we
might need one. Your kindness is always
very much appreciated and never taken
for granted."

"It's been such good fun," Rachel replied, pinning on her badge. "We've really enjoyed helping you all."

"We're always happy to help our fairy friends," Kirsty added with a smile. "All you have to do is ask."

The Helping Fairies gathered around them for a big group hug, and then Queen Titania spoke again.

"I think you should be getting back to the human world, girls," she said with a smile. "I believe that you have a ceremony to attend."

Among a fluttering of sparkles, the girls watched as the Throne Room disappeared and was replaced by the tiled walls of the swimming pool. They were human again and back in their swimming costumes, standing beside the

pool. The goblins had vanished. Mark
was standing at the deep end, and as the
girls watched he performed a smooth
dive into the water. Then he swam several
laps up and down the pool, cutting
through the water with great speed and
grace.

"He's remembered how to swim," said
Rachel with a smile.

"Thanks to Lulu," Kirsty added.

Mark saw them and climbed out, smiling.

"I'm glad you're still here, girls," he said. "I don't know what came over me earlier, but everything is back to normal now. Let everyone know that the lesson is going to go ahead after all!"

That evening, Tippington Town Hall was packed with people. The nominees for the Tippington Helper of the Year Award had helped so many people that they could hardly all squeeze in! Kirsty was sitting close to the front with Rachel and her parents, waiting for the mayor to announce the winner. The girls reached for each other's hand as they watched the mayor open a golden envelope. Their hearts were racing.

"I am absolutely delighted to announce that this year's Tippington Helper of the Year Award goes to…Lesley Walker!" she declared. "Many congratulations!"

"YES!" shouted the girls, jumping to their feet.

Looking very pink-cheeked, Aunt Lesley got up to receive her award.

Rachel and Kirsty's hands hurt from clapping so hard! At the end of her thank you speech, she smiled down at the girls and then gazed around the room.

"As grateful as I am, I would like to remind everyone that all everyday heroes are important," she said. "I would like to share this award with the other nominees. Mark the lifeguard, Isobel the firefighter and Colin the paramedic help people every day of their lives, and they deserve this award every bit as much as I do. Please come and join me."

The audience cheered and whistled as the others made their way up to the stage. Aunt Lesley, Mark, Isobel and Colin smiled around at the people they had helped, and Rachel and Kirsty looked down at the special badges that the fairies had given them.

"I'm so happy that we were able to help the fairies get their magical objects back from Jack Frost and his goblins," said Kirsty.

"Me too," said Rachel. "I wonder when we'll have another chance to help them."

"Soon, I hope," said Kirsty. "Helping others feels really good!"

Meet the Storybook Fairies

Can Rachel and Kirsty help get their new fairy friends'
magical objects back from Jack Frost, before all
their favourite stories are ruined?

www.rainbowmagicbooks.co.uk

**Now it's time for Kirsty and
Rachel to help...**

Alyssa the Snow Queen Fairy

Read on for a sneak peek...

"What an icy, grey December this is,"
said Rachel Walker, blowing on her
fingers and shivering. "I'm starting to
wonder if Christmas will ever arrive!"

It was Saturday morning, and Rachel
was in her garden with her best friend,
Kirsty Tate. They had come out to play
a game of ball, but the sleet was getting
heavier. Kirsty shivered too, and buried
her hands deep in her pockets.

"I'm really glad to be staying with you
for the weekend, but I wish the weather
wasn't so horrible," she said.

"We had such lovely things planned,"

said Rachel. "But nature walks and boating on the lake won't be much fun when it's so grey and freezing. It looks as if we'll be spending most of the weekend inside."

"Never mind," said Kirsty, grinning at her friend. "We always have fun when we're together, no matter what we're doing."

"You're right," said Rachel, trying to forget about the dark clouds above.

"Perhaps we should go inside," Kirsty said. "I think it's starting to snow."

"Oh, really?" said Rachel, feeling more cheerful. "Maybe we can go sledging."

"I don't think so," said Kirsty. "I can only see one snowflake."

She pointed up to the single, perfect snowflake. It was spiralling down from the grey sky. The girls watched it land on the edge of a stone birdbath.

"That's funny," said Rachel after a moment. "It's not melting."

Kirsty took a step closer to the birdbath. "I think it's getting bigger," she said.

Read **Alyssa the Snow Queen Fairy** to find out what adventures are in store for Kirsty and Rachel!

Calling all parents, carers and teachers!
The Rainbow Magic fairies are here to help
your child enter the magical world of reading.
Whatever reading stage they are at, there's
a Rainbow Magic book for everyone!
Here is Lydia the Reading Fairy's guide to
supporting your child's journey at all levels.

Starting Out
Our Rainbow Magic Beginner Readers are perfect for first-time readers who are just beginning to develop reading skills and confidence. Approved by teachers, they contain a full range of educational levelling, as well as lively full-colour illustrations.

Developing Readers
Rainbow Magic Early Readers contain longer stories and wider vocabulary for building stamina and growing confidence. These are adaptations of our most popular Rainbow Magic stories, specially developed for younger readers in conjunction with an Early Years reading consultant, with full-colour illustrations.

Going Solo
The Rainbow Magic chapter books – a mixture of series and one-off specials – contain accessible writing to encourage your child to venture into reading independently. These highly collectible and much-loved magical stories inspire a love of reading to last a lifetime.

www.rainbowmagicbooks.co.uk

"Rainbow Magic got my daughter reading chapter books. Great sparkly covers, cute fairies and traditional stories full of magic that she found impossible to put down" – Mother of Edie (6 years)

"Florence LOVES the Rainbow Magic books. She really enjoys reading now" Mother of Florence (6 years)

Read along the Reading Rainbow!

Well done – you have completed the book!

This book was worth 1 star.

See how far you have climbed on the Reading Rainbow.
The more books you read, the more stars you can colour in
and the closer you will be to becoming a Royal Fairy!

Do you want to print your own Reading Rainbow?

1) Go to the Rainbow Magic website

2) Download and print out the poster

3) Colour in a star for every book you finish
and climb the Reading Rainbow

4) For every step up the rainbow,
you can download your very own certificate

There's all this and lots more at
rainbowmagicbooks.co.uk

You'll find activities, stories, a special newsletter
AND you can search for the fairy with your name!

TRIGGERPRESS

Giving mental health a voice

www.trigger-press.com

For anyone who's ever been labelled a "whiny needy twerp" or an "attention seeking bastard" for bravely battling mental illness.

INTRODUCTION

Apologies if I offend anyone here, but I don't actually believe stigmata exists. I know there are drawings of it in the Bible and everything, but I'm not sure anyone has ever been treated for *actual* stigmata of the biblical type. It is not a contributing factor to the NHS crisis, as far as I'm aware.

I know I'm treading a precarious path here, especially given the recent allegations about Stephen Fry's apparent illegal blasphemy.[1] Whoopsie daisy, Mr Fry – how very dare you?!

But there, I said it. I don't believe in stigmata. Not now, anyway.

Back in the 90s, however, American movie star Patricia Arquette made me believe otherwise, albeit briefly.

I've always been drawn to horror movies. I don't know why, given that I'm an absolute wuss who still gets frightened watching *Ghostbusters* (remember the old lady in the library? You can't argue with that).

Anyway, *Stigmata* with Patricia Arquette was one movie that I enjoyed in the late 90s. I say enjoyed – I watched it and, without letting on to my then boyfriend (who had his feet up on the sofa, completely unaware), I discreetly checked my hands and feet for bloody holes. An all-too-familiar feeling of dread hit me.

---

1 Stephen Fry went onto TV in 2015 and asked, 'Why should I respect a capricious, mean-minded, stupid god who creates a world which is so full of injustice and pain?'

Hidden by the side of the armchair, my fingertips secretly wandered over the centre of my palms. I expected my fingertips to disappear into a bloody void. They didn't, of course.

I checked my feet. They were safely snuggled up in my stripy slipper socks. My blood was not seeping through. How could I be sure, though, that I wasn't bleeding underneath the fabric? These were high quality socks! How could I check my feet without my boyfriend seeing me and realising that his girlfriend was completely crazy – or worse still, possessed?

It's amazing how you can convince yourself that your hand aches just by thinking about it.

Nothing came of it that night, but it didn't stop me, days and even weeks later, typing "stigmata" into Google and hitting the search button.

Oh. My. God. Stigmata phenomena had indeed been reported. That was no movie. That was on the internet. *It must be true*, I thought. After all, the internet was my new go-to place for facts, wasn't it?

I can't pretend, even today, that I am not slightly nervous writing about this topic, in case the spiritual world picks up on it and inflicts stigmata as a punishment for committing blasphemy or being an unbeliever.

But no. Hang on just a moment. That won't happen. It's all me, after all. The ache I felt in my hands was borne of my own anxious brain and Patricia Arquette's scary movie scenes.

Let's look at it in the cold light of day. What really is stigmata?

Stigmata. Awful bloody marks that Jesus found in his hands and feet after being nailed to the cross. A punishment.

Stigma. Simply, a mark of disgrace.

Thinking I could have stigmata left a mark of disgrace – a mark I put there myself for feeling so embarrassed about my anxious thoughts.

Was I going mad? I must have been. I was either crazy or possessed. I didn't much fancy either.

It's funny how the world sometimes encourages me and my brain to wish all this stuff on myself. It feels like anxiety makes me weak. And sickly. And crazy. And a failure.

It's probably no surprise that one of my favourite teenage songs was 'Crucify' by Tori Amos. Listening to that song overindulged my adolescent bent towards self-punishment. Because let's face it – as a British teenager in the 90s, I wasn't spending my Saturday nights with 90's pop princess Whigfield, a mirror, and a hairbrush, like a lot of other girls. Instead I was chasing the romantic notion of having a dark and twisted existence. And in the 80s you were usually one kind of teenager or the other (labels, again).

But Jesus! (Sorry). We've got to stop all this. There are enough people in the world giving us a kicking without us doing it ourselves. Which is worse – the world calling me crazy and weak, or my belief that I am crazy or weak? The two go hand in hand, but the latter is more damaging. After all, if your mind is feeling vulnerable because you're beating yourself up, it will believe the shite pedalled by ignorant tossers on social media. And it will stop you getting help, lowering your anxiety levels or simply just getting it off your chest. If only Piers Morgan and Katie Hopkins would shut the fuck up for a change, then perhaps another like-minded individual wouldn't hide their anxieties from their nearest and dearest. Perhaps they wouldn't have to stay silent. Perhaps they wouldn't feel ashamed.

Hmm ... marks of disgrace. They're everywhere. Hopkins and Morgan seem to revel in driving the nails in. But we shouldn't hold our hands out for them, or indeed anyone else.

You see, we're scoring too many own goals. We need to see these perceptions for what they really are. We need to give ourselves a well-earned break. None of this stigma and self-stigma stuff has any real substance. It's time we vaporised it all, over a hot steaming mug of camomile tea. We need to see it for what it is and laugh at the sheer ridiculousness of it.

Fancy joining me? Cool! Grab the biscuit tin, put your feet up and let's pick those self-inflicted stereotypes apart one by one, until we can finally say 'Stigma? What a load of old shit!'

Self-stigma

But first, let's start by looking at what self-stigma is. Basically, it's the internalised impact of what the outside world tells us. I know about this, because I have experienced it first-hand.

It's borne of some of the stigmatising things we experience at the hands of others. These things can be the very source of our own irrational thinking when it comes to mental illness. Somebody pierces our wrists with a nasty insult or a negative idea, and we continue to twist the rusty nails until they're embedded in our very being.

I must add a very important disclaimer. I'm not a psychologist. I haven't a psychology GCSE to my name. I own the odd variation on *Psychology for Dummies* but as far as academia goes, a D in A Level Art is the closest I'm going to get.

But it's easy to label things, isn't it? To pluck a word from the vast and growing English language to describe someone or something?

That guy is so OCD.

She's so schizophrenic. She can never make her mind up.

Ugh, he's such a depressive.

Illnesses have become adjectives. Illnesses of the mind, anyway. Either that, or a person becomes the illness itself. But try it with a physical illness; it won't seem so familiar:

Ugh, she's doing my head in. She's such an overactive thyroid.

Nope. Never heard that one.

There's this special and mysterious book called the *Diagnostic Statistical Manual of Mental Disorders*. I believe psychiatrists use it – and I believe they diagnose their patients with care and caution. Now,

I know there's a big bad fight between psychiatrists and psychologists on this subject of labelling and handing out diagnoses. I've seen it on Twitter. But I'd like to avoid that debate for now, if that's okay.

But hey, who cares, the unqualified Joe Public has a voice and a load of social media channels from which to yell, so let's all sling a few diagnoses at people on Twitter and see what happens. I mean, you don't need a qualification to know that your workmate's "a bit OCD" right?

There's a big movement of people who campaign against mental health stigma – through the national Time to Change campaign and beyond. And that's bloody important. Why? Because stigma translates into self-stigma, a topic less often discussed.

If your brain's a bit poorly, self-stigma is a terribly dangerous thing. It comes from those pedalling stigma and stereotypes all around us, but it also comes from within ourselves and everything we've learnt over the years. It comes from the anxieties we carry on our backs every single day.

Tragically, and infuriatingly, self-stigma doesn't need to happen. But more and more we find people pushing stigma and using it to bait those with mental illness, to raise a level of controversy that boosts their profiles.

We all love to boo a pantomime baddie, but that's usually because they're stealing a magic lamp or weaving destructive magic spells. We know it's all made up and we know they'll get their comeuppance. Yet public figures like Hopkins and Morgan appear to enjoy the boos and hisses. They bring pantomime into real life. They bait us with mental health stigma. Sadly, that's not fiction.

For example, a tweet from Piers Morgan about the singer Will Young said, "Will Young does not have PTSD. He has WNTS – Whiny Needy Twerp Syndrome."

It was a reaction to Will Young's interview with writer and journalist Bryony Gordon for the *Telegraph*. And I'm not naïve; I've served my time working in PR. I get that there is always a reason for why things are said. I get that Piers Morgan may not even wholeheartedly believe his own tweet (it's a possibility). But if that is the case, it's even worse. It's baiting and ridiculing people with mental illness to enhance Piers Morgan's brand. And that cannot contribute to the wellbeing of British society.

And TV personality Katie Hopkins? Following Prince Harry's interview with Bryony Gordon, Hopkins' *Daily Mail* column was headlined with the following:

I'm sorry, but I LIKE my royals calm, cold and ever-so-slightly heartless – not oversharing their issues like a guest on Loose Women.

And these two are just the tip of the iceberg.

Of course, the mentally ill are fair game, aren't they? They're bound to get upset and have a tantrum. That'll get the Twitter engagement figures flying. That'll land more controversial headlines.

Denise Welch, a popular UK actress, rightly called out the lovely Piers Morgan for his Will Young tweet, which resulted in more mud-slinging. Piers called Denise a "publicity-starved bore." Nice.

So why am I falling into their trap and talking about them some more? Why am I contributing to the immortalisation of the tweet and the headline?

Because they already have the platform and the airtime. They already have the ears and eyes of millions of people. And they already have the power to influence. They need to be challenged.

They're already out there and they're already reaching millions of people. At least if I repeat it in *my* words I can throw my own context around it – like many other like-minded campaigners and writers have.

The pedalling of mental health stigma, something that the Time to Change campaign has been fighting for years, doesn't just create pantomime-style rows on Twitter. It goes beyond that. And the rows go beyond Piers vs. Denise too. I saw so many Piers Morgan supporters attacking the "trend" of mental illness, some claiming that mental illness wasn't even around in the 60s and 70s. They said it's a new thing. Some said, in line with Katie Hopkins' opinion about Prince Harry speaking out, that they preferred the "stiff upper lip" approach to life.

So imagine this. You're a man in your thirties. You've been struggling to get out of bed in the morning. Your mood has dropped. You can't concentrate at work and you're making mistakes. Your boss has noticed that you've been consistently late recently, because you're not sleeping properly.

You're starting to contemplate the idea that you might, possibly, have a mental illness.

You go onto Twitter to check your notifications. You see that Will Young has been called "whiny". You see people saying the Brits should bring back their "stiff upper lip" approach to life. You see people arguing that mental illness is just an excuse for everyday challenges in life.

You think, *Christ, I need to pull myself together*. This is ridiculous. *I don't have a mental health problem*.

You get up for work the next day, but you're really struggling now. You chastise yourself for considering that your laziness could really be a health problem. You're unable to speak coherently in meetings. It brings on panic. Every time you need to speak to people you get heart palpitations and sweat profusely. You start skipping meetings.

But you can't go to the doctor. You need to be strong. And you certainly can't say anything at work. They'd think you were weak, just like everyone says on Twitter.

Things get worse and worse. You receive a final warning from your boss. You lose your job. Now there's nothing to get out of bed for. You feel guilty for being so weak that you hide away from your friends and family. Your money troubles get worse. You can't eat properly and your physical health starts to fail. Your mortgage payment is late ...

You can see where I'm going with this. The "stiff upper lip" approach is dangerous. But big influencers like Piers Morgan and Katie Hopkins push it out for all it's worth. And the media gives them an even bigger platform from which to shout it out, loudly – even mainstream morning television, for God's sake.

So, there is a reason for bringing this up. And it's not to create more headlines for Piers and Katie, but it's in the hope that people see how dangerous their attention grabbing controversy really is. It's in the hope that somebody will take responsibility for putting this stuff out there.

Provoking mental health stigma might put Piers and Katie in the headlines, but it has the power to put other people in hospital. Or worse. And we need to remember that. The media outlets that give them the platforms need to remember that it's a double-edged sword. Their ratings might go up, but that actually creates an even bigger health risk for society. Do they really want to be responsible for that?

These damaging attitudes towards mental health make us feel weak, crazy or dramatic. They make us feel like it's our own fault if we end up in A&E with yet another health scare at 11.30pm on a Friday night. (Because of course we're delighted to spend our Friday night in A&E wasting public money and resources. God, we're so selfish.)

We often internalise these attitudes and make ourselves feel ridiculous and useless and stupid, when we already have troubling thoughts racing around our heads. Stigma stops us speaking about our illnesses or sometimes even seeking help from doctors. Damaging attitudes can even stop us believing there's anything wrong in the first place.

Self-stigma is a bitch.

I'm not ashamed to admit that I have engaged in self-stigma over the years. I grew up thinking I lived near a "nut house" (because that's what we ignorantly called it in the 90s) and I have since chided myself for behaving like a "nutter", "lunatic" and "crazy bitch".

I've gone on to realise that I was ill. I have sought help, I have spoken out and then I have chided myself again for being "weak", an "attention seeker", and a "drama queen". I've convinced myself that I made up all this anxiety bollocks. *What a load of old shit! What the hell have I got to be anxious about, anyway?*

And then I was hit slap bang in the face with some serious stigma and discrimination (which, for legal reasons, I'll be suitably vague about). So I started writing about mental health and stigma – blogging about it, speaking out in the media, joining peer support groups at work. It was a big step, putting myself out there – warts and all – for the world to see. But I felt compelled to do it. And it was kind of cathartic too.

I nervously set up my blog, drafted my first piece, and hit the publish button. And waited, nervously and anxiously (surprise, surprise). I linked it to Twitter and then to Facebook.

What was the world going to think? That I needed attention? That I was being one of those dramatic types that writes mysterious posts about having a terrible day, to try to entice my Facebook friends into asking what's up? That I would eventually give in and say 'Oh, it's nothing really, don't worry. I just got fed up with Vodafone keeping me on hold for seven minutes'?

All this panic was whirred through my brain. But then the comments started. The private messages started pinging through. And they weren't accusing me of being an attention seeking diva – far from it. I had messages from old school friends who I hadn't spoken to in years, telling me they were so pleased that I shared the post because they'd been suffering from a similar illness and they hadn't dared speak out about it. Others said they were glad that it wasn't just them. Some publicly commented and shared their own experiences. And then others joined in on the comments thread and everyone was positive and supportive and happy.

Of course, there may have been others who did, offline, comment on my whiny neediness, but who cares when the public comments were so positive?

So I took it a step further and applied to take part in the Time to Change StoryCamp. For those who don't know it, Time to Change is a national stigma-busting campaign run by Mind and Rethink Mental Illness. And StoryCamp? Well, that's a blogger event that they set up to encourage more people like me, with lived experience of mental ill health, to share their story. I applied, I got through and I whizzed off to London to meet more like-minded peeps who were ready and willing to speak out.

Woohoo! I've done it. I'm a crusader on a mission. I'm She-Ra, the Princess of Power, fighting against evil in Stereotype City. I'm part of the great big Time to Change movement that practically defined this mission, handed us all maps and sent us out into the big bad world to promote goodness and virtue.

Hang on a minute. Have I let this go to my head? Am I enjoying the attention a bit too much? Am I a narcissist? A great big, self-obsessed, fame-seeking, big-headed narcissist?!

CHAPTER 1

Stereotype: The Narcissist

REALITY: THE SELF-LOATHER

Stereotype number one: narcissism. Let's get this one out of the way first because, after all, I'm writing about myself here. And if we don't tackle this subject and agree on a conclusion, then you might not like me. And I really, really want you to like me (in fact, try replacing "want" with "need").

Since I started on my blogging vanity trip, I have often pondered this one. Well, I say pondered – more like obsessively agonised over it. Am I simply a self-promoting, narcissistic Twitter whore who simply cannot bear to go unnoticed?

I mean, I bleat relentlessly on social media about who has complimented my work, who has given me a testimonial, who has published me, how many likes I've had and how many times my article has been shared.

Look at me. Listen to me. I'm just bloody fantastic, me. I bet you can't get enough of me.

It's not quite as simple as that, though.

This apparent vanity – when exactly is it authentic? If you could peer into my soul, would you find it lurking in the deepest, darkest depths of my personality? Or is it as shallow as the symptoms that ooze from it? I need other people to praise me because, let's be honest, I'm really not very good at it myself. Without those little nuggets of reassurance, I'm not exactly what you might call confident.

The problem is, those little nuggets of reassurance are transient, fleeting, temporary little teasers that go in one ear and then out the other. You can't catch them and build them up into one great big dollop of self-esteem, because they haven't come from within in the first place. You don't truly believe them. It's fucking exhausting. The reason I want people to like my blogs, articles, and tweets is because I need to know that they're not a pile of poop, not because I need to know that they are life-changing. But if someone were to tell me that one of my articles was life-changing, then that's a solid reason to believe that my writing isn't utter bollocks and I am not completely talentless.

Perhaps Carly Simon's song should have gone: *You're so paranoid / I bet you think this song is about you*. The result is the same.

I've heard the word "egotist" used about anxious people on more than one occasion. Oh, did I not mention my diagnosis? Yep – I myself am one of those anxious peeps. I have Generalised Anxiety Disorder. It's not a label that was thrown at me from every direction. It was actually only suggested to me in 2016 – by my fifth counsellor.

Before understanding that my anxiety was generalised, I thought it had more of a niche. I thought I was only anxious about my health. Maybe that felt more manageable, more special, more exclusive. Anyway, I eventually realised that my anxiety didn't sign up to any particular theme. It just wasn't that fussy.

Everyone's staring at me. Everyone hates me. Nobody likes my writing. Everyone thinks I'm ugly. They're all talking behind my back. Were they laughing at me just then? Was that comment aimed at me?

The person who thinks everyone spends every waking hour bitching about them is not necessarily a raging egotist. They might, however, be an extremely anxious or depressed person.

This is probably why that Carly Simon song has always infuriated me. Thinking a song is about you might not necessarily be a symptom of vanity, but of insecurity.

And if we look to the darker world of grunge, we find a less comfortable, more edgy sound of "paranoia"– something a little more apt for a teenager of the early 90s like me. I remember thinking that Nirvana's 'In Bloom' was written about me. I thought Kurt Cobain knew that I, as an individual, was a fraud. Yes – I'm so "egotistical", I believed that one of the biggest bands in the world used me as a muse. For a song. About people being fake and just not getting it. That's not vanity, really, is it?

I no longer fit in the grownup grunge scene, but there is one place I do fit: the mental health community. The Time to Change crusaders. There's loads of them and they're all doing great work.

But, hang on a minute (again). Am I just jumping on the bandwagon? Do I really have a proper mental health problem? Have I made it up to get attention? Is this just the narcissist in me?

People have come out in droves and started speaking out about their experiences. But other people are speaking out now too: the trolls. They say we are trying to make mental health trendy.

In the 80s, it was Simon le Bon's frilly shirt. In the 90s, it was Jennifer Aniston's hair. Today, it's Zayn Malik's anxiety. Celebrities all over the world have been spotted flouting their latest fashion accessory – the mental health diagnosis.

NB: I made this headline up.

It's like shopping with ASOS (otherwise known as "As Seen on Screen" – a shopper's guide to dressing like the stars). Zayn Malik's got anxiety, so apparently I want a piece of the action. Really? When people speak out about cancer or heart disease, we don't accuse them of trying to make the illness "trendy". However, those who speak out about mental health are sometimes criticised for that very reason. On Twitter, for example:

"Mental health disorders are not something to brag about. Please stop trying to make mental illness trendy."

"Having mental health issues is now trendy, the new victim fad."

Sadly, my own anxiety disorder has outlived the puffball dress and the spiral perm. It appears to be a "trend" that has stood the test of time. I haven't chosen to be trendy with my anxiety accessory. And no matter how hard I try, I can't seem to shake it off. Wouldn't it be nice if you could get rid of it with a new hair dye or a change in fashion sense?

It's a similar story with celebrity mental health ambassadors. They don't just "try it on" for the sake of the latest campaign.

In fact, long before celebrities signed up as mental health ambassadors, many were unwillingly "outed" by the media, with headlines boasting "sensational" photos of them breaking down in public.

Actress Denise Welch is just one celebrity who has been subjected to her fair share of media shaming. In fact, she still is. Before becoming a mental health campaigner, she was constantly appearing in "shocking" reports and "exclusive" photos relating to her drinking binges. In the end, she spoke out about her struggles with clinical depression and how she self-medicated with alcohol – the very thing that the media was taking the piss out of her for. That's like having a pop at someone for wearing a cast over a broken leg.

Only recently, one magazine turned Denise's support for the Heads Together mental health campaign into another "sensational", attention grabbing headline – and not in a good way. She had spoken out about her mental health for the launch of the campaign. It was a touching film showing Denise in conversation with her husband, Lincoln Townley. They spoke openly and candidly and lovingly. I was so touched watching them that by the end of the film, mascara-filled tears were streaming down my face.

At one point, Denise shared her early concerns from when they first met. She was worried about telling Lincoln about the extent of her mental health problems.

So how did the magazine translate it? It was something along the lines of *Denise Welch's Marriage Crisis*. Yep – they actually turned the above scenario into a headline that hinted at a possible break up. Jesus.

I'm sure Denise isn't doing all this mental health work simply to boost her own profile, not when she's lumbered with crap like that as part of the package. And also, if she does find some catharsis in speaking out – if it helps Denise as much as it helps the wider public – then what's wrong with that?

So, those accusations of attention seeking and jumping on the mental health bandwagon? They're rubbish!

I remember somebody messaging me to say thank you for sharing my experience, as it inspired them to book a counselling appointment. The negativity I encounter (or often imagine I encounter – because that happens too) pales in comparison when I hear feedback like that. And, ironically, the longer people complain about mental illness being "on trend", the longer we will struggle with it. It is talked about so proactively precisely *because* of these negative attitudes.

The trend will only go away when the stigma does. Only when it's treated with the same respect as physical health will the "trendy" ambassadors finally put their feet up and say 'Job done.' I don't think that will happen any time soon, sadly.

So, you do need to build up some degree of resilience to be a mental health advocate. I've seen all the negative tweets and I try to ignore them. But what about the nagging voices that shout at me from inside my own head?

Although I've seen the tweets, I haven't actually seen any *specifically* targeted at me. It feels like they are, though. And I can easily turn that kind of stigma into something personal, by internalising it and soaking it all up like a sponge.

Self-stigma can either stop you from continuing in your mental health battle or, at worst, make you feel really, really down. Neither option is helpful.

And anyway, if your self-esteem is low, and you can do something – maybe something you're talented at – to make you feel a bit better about yourself, then why the hell not?

Of course you're worthy of wearing the Princess of Power crown! That doesn't make you a narcissist or an attention seeker!

Why should we feel guilty for climbing up onto our own pedestals from time to time and taking in the view? Especially when we've never really done it before. We tend to lift everyone else around us up there instead, and then look up to them, green with envy.

So whether you're good at writing, cooking, drawing, sports, mechanics, having the business sense of Richard Branson or being an empathetic support worker – your talents are really important and there's no shame in talking about them. Find them in your recovery and you'll set off on a positive journey with a strong sense of direction. Pat yourself on the back for a change – it doesn't make you Narcissus to acknowledge what you're good at.

Want me to prove it? Okay, let's take a look at who Narcissus was meant to be and what he was really all about.

If you haven't heard the tale, it goes a little something like this:

Narcissus was a hunter from Greek mythology who was known for his beauty. However, Nemesis noticed that he was proud as punch for all the admiration he received. To teach him a lesson, he lured Narcissus to a pool of water in which he could see his own reflection. There, at the pool, Narcissus caught a glimpse of his boyband looks and instantly fell in love with himself, unable to leave the pool of water ever again. He sat by that pool until he died.

Anyway, that's Narcissus. I don't imagine many people reading this will identify. Here's why.

1. Would Narcissus have placed anyone but himself on a pedestal?

If I was seriously as arrogant as Narcissus, would I be that impressed that Sarah Millican had shared my article on Facebook once? Hmm ... possibly not, because I would probably think that I was at least on the same level as her. So, being really flattered that somebody you deem to be more talented than you liked your post doesn't really make you narcissistic, does it? I find it quite humbling, actually.

2. Could Narcissus see his own flaws, let alone share them with the world?

Now, considering Narcissus had a puddle of water for a mirror, I doubt he would have had the means to share his immense brilliance with the world via BT infinity and social media. But still, in his naturally occurring aquatic mirror, he couldn't see the monstrous yellow boil he had on his face, or the slimy green snot hanging off his nose (yes, I'm using artistic licence to make a point).

But I see my flaws. Boy, do I see them. And I tell the world about them (well, maybe not the world, but a handful of people who follow my blog). I have serious insecurities. I constantly wish I was as pretty or talented or popular or confident as everyone else on Facebook. I have a major obsession with the shape of my jaw that has led me to spend a ridiculous amount of time googling (and seriously considering) surgery options for many years. My voice makes me sound weak, my eyes disappear when I smile and my legs will never be long / slim / smooth / tanned enough to bare. I do spend a lot of time staring in the mirror, but what I see is very different to what Narcissus saw. We know that the selfie revolution isn't based on confidence, now, don't we?

3. Narcissus was known for his beauty and hunting skills.

I was known for being self-absorbed, overly emotional and destructive. (Remember that minor issue of discrimination I mentioned earlier? Well, while in the midst of an anxiety relapse, that is exactly how someone described me. Nice.)

So forgive me if I am over-egging the pudding of mild success. But when you've been told that your very personality is one seriously major flaw, a little bit of self-promotion is kind of understandable. I worked in PR for years. I constantly promoted other people, other organisations, other things. And then I found something that I might be a bit good at and enjoy doing (writing).

Self-affirmation? Why the hell not?

4. Staring in a pool of water until you die helps nobody.

But blogging about mental health does. I've received so many messages saying that by talking openly about my experiences, others have felt "more normal" and that "it's okay" to have a mental health problem. They've even told me that they might even start writing about theirs too. I mean, I remember my good friend Paul telling me that he thought he was going to end up as some sort of medical experiment until he read Geri Halliwell's book about her own anxiety and mental health. Yes – he was in fact saved by a Spice Girl (that's got to be the title of your autobiography, right Paul?)

But all this aside, while I'm certainly no raging Narcissus, I think I possibly am *fairly* narcissistic at times.

But do we actually understand what that means? Mine is a thin and brittle mask that hides a vulnerable soul. It's kind of like a precarious sinkhole on the motorway, waiting to fall in. Scratch the surface a little too hard and my insecurity will eventually be exposed. I don't think it's an enviable position to be in.

In fact, I think we are all a little narcissistic at times. I believe I sway from one of end of the narcissism scale to the other – introverted to extroverted. Occasionally, I'm in the healthy zone.

If I have understood this correctly, introverted narcissism is where you strive to be something you're not and punish yourself when you don't make it. You therefore never feel good enough because you believe you *should* be a superstar and you just don't make the grade. Extroverted narcissism is when you want to share your greatness with the world.

As I stated at the beginning, I am not a professional on these subjects. But I hope that I have grasped the basics. If you want to understand more on this subject, however, grab a copy of *The Narcissist Test* by Dr Craig Malkin. He's quite the authority on the topic.

I remember feeling like a complete failure in my late twenties because I hadn't made an impact on the world like Madonna did in the 80s. I hadn't set the scene; I'd only followed it. Seriously. I worried I was going to die having been nothing but a marketing manager. I would not have an obituary in *The Times*. Nobody would talk about the contribution I made to the world.

Self-obsessed much? Yes, probably, but it is entirely driven by feelings of sheer inadequacy.

I remember when my wonderful husband suggested I was getting good at running and that I should enter the Great North Run. My response astounded him. 'No,' I said. 'Because I won't win it.' Of course I wouldn't have won. Elite athletes run in the Great North Run. I watched with envy one year as people I knew took to Facebook to post their finish times for the race. They were part of something. We saw the pictures of them gearing up at the starting line and then – the hardest part for me – we saw them posting their brilliant finish times.

I, on the other hand, scared of being outdone by everyone else, set off on my own run on the same day. I managed 11.1 miles – just two short of the half marathon. I had never, ever run that far in my life. What an accomplishment.

No, it wasn't. I calculated my average and worked out that even at my two miles short of the Great North Run, my pace was lagging behind those of my Facebook friends.

It was a personal best for me, but a disappointment in comparison to others. And that was all that mattered.

Nothing is ever good enough. It's not a great place to be.

My other half is *terribly* shy of self-promotion. He's an actor, so in reality, he needs to be good at self-promotion. He's a great actor (and not just in my opinion – check out the reviews! Google Chris Connel – #proudwife) but he wouldn't feel comfortable telling the world that he is. So after a talking-to from his marketing-obsessed wife (me), he had a crack at it. After all, if you're a self-employed actor you've got to do your own marketing.

So one day, instead of posting his scathing opinion on Theresa May or a link to a film entitled *12 Hilarious Times People Fell Off Stuff*, he updated his profile with a summary of the new projects he was working on. He couldn't believe the response he got. That status had far more likes than the one where he shared *YouTube's Epic Fails Part III*. He hadn't expected that. Nobody thought bad of him for feeling a little bit of pride and sharing it.

So unless you've reached the highly distracting levels of self-adoration endured by Narcissus, don't feel bad about it. You are not Narcissus. Understanding and recognising your strengths is surely the only way to grow, to succeed. After all, you rarely get a job without submitting a CV and bragging about why you're the best person for the job at interview.

However, it would be lovely not to need this form of external validation. It's tiring having to constantly seek it out and we know that we can never keep hold of it. It always slips through the net.

I really hope that, by the time I've finished writing this book, I reach a point where I am far less reliant on external validation. I hope I reach a point where I can start looking to myself for validation rather than to other people. I want to believe in, and trust, my own worth. That's what I'm working on with counsellor number six anyway.

And think about it – the more you focus on your strengths, the less you'll think about your weaknesses, your faults, your anxieties, your imperfections, your blemishes ... your ...

Ooh ... what's that red mark on my arm? It wasn't there before ...

CHAPTER 2

Stereotype: The Hypochondriac

REALITY: THE POORLY MIND

Shit. I've got DVT. Shit. Shit. Shit. I can't breathe properly.

The pill, plus smoking Embassy Number 1, plus having sex, plus being me, plus drinking that Mad Dog 20/20 last week – it all adds up!

I shouldn't be having sex. I'm 15. I shouldn't be smoking. My Grandma had cancer. It's in the family. I'M GOING TO GET CANCER!

I'm going to die young. And not in a rock star kind of way.

I've got to get to the payphone. I've got to ring my mum. I can't see properly.

I feel faint. The railings. The road, get over the road. In the payphone. Dial. Breathe. I can't breathe.

'Mum. It's me. I think I've got DVT. Well there's a red mark on my arm and I'm on the pi— why wouldn't you be able to see it? Well, what is it then?! ... Oh ... Right ... I still feel funny though. My heart feels funny. Will you come and get me? Okay, thanks. See you in a bit. Bye.'

My vision has gone. My legs have gone. I can't breathe properly. If it's not DVT then what the actual fuck is this?

I can't breathe. I can't slow down. I can't breathe.

I'm going to be sick.

My first realisation of panic. I was 15.

I loved staying at my boyfriend's bedsit in Hull, mainly because we used to nip down to the chippy where my 15-year-old vegetarian self (you carry a lot of guilt at that age – just like Tori Amos) routinely ordered chips and a cheese 'n' onion pattie[2] – often topped with scraps. We'd flick on the telly and watch one of the four options open to us ... (probably a toss-up between *Brookside*, *A Question of Sport*, *Murder Most Horrid* and *You've Been Framed*. A world without Netflix).

But one day, even with all the usual early evening decadence to look forward to, something went wrong. We hadn't even plated up the chips when I spotted a little red mark on my arm.

2 A deep fried 'pattie' consisting of mashed potato and sage – sometimes with added ingredients – often found in Hull's finest chip shops!

It took a dash to the payphone and a five-minute chat with my very understanding mother to talk me out of the inexplicable conclusion I had made, in a matter of 0.37 seconds, since first noticing the sinister little mark. However, after I put the receiver down, my body was still doing some very strange things and I literally found myself crawling on all fours, clinging to the railings and praying nobody I knew could see me.

I realised that it was in fact a panic attack. I realised this because it happened again, when I got out of the bath and found a lump in my groin. And again, when I was shopping in Tesco and found a rash on my arm. And again, when I felt a tightness in my calf that was surely DVT (deep vein thrombosis). Again.

It was about a year later when the phantom DVT struck again. I had a new teenage boyfriend and I was on the escalator in Princes Quay shopping centre in Hull, heading up towards the top deck where everyone hung out around Kingston Jeanery and Leonardo's coffee shop. My leg began to ache. I was back in the now all-too-familiar zone …

DVT! It must be! I can't say anything. My boyfriend and his brother will think I'm weird. What if it's nothing? But WHAT IF IT'S DVT? It can go to your heart. And your lungs. And you can die. What if my vision goes funny again? What if I pass out?

I calmed down a little until we got to the charity shop where his mum was working.

The ache is back. I'm too embarrassed to say anything. My insides are knotted and I need to look cool and I'm already shy and awkward and now they're ALL going to think I'm really REALLY weird and stupid and shy. I so don't want to be shy. I so don't want to die. Not here, not with people I don't really know. I CANNOT collapse here in the charity shop among the teasmades and old lady anoraks. Can you imagine what the Hull Daily Mail would say? I might even wet myself. They'll report it. L7 might throw tampons into crowds of fans and Courtney Love might sing about being a teenage whore – but they choose to do that. And I bet they've never bloody wet themselves. That's not out of control. That's loss of control.

These experiences were definitely panic attacks. I knew that much. But I had no idea that it was a mental illness. Back then, I thought mental illness was having hallucinations and talking to yourself and all that "crazy shit" (more stigma). I had no idea that my problems were a form of mental illness.

And even when I racked up the A&E visits and the GP consultations and the counselling sessions, I still didn't really understand that I had a mental health problem.

'Lucy, they're your glands, not cancerous lumps.'

'Lucy, you have scratched and bruised yourself. You do not have meningitis.'

'Lucy, when your feet went numb how were you sitting? Were you on your knees? That will explain things ...'

'Lucy, you do not have bowel cancer; your stomach is simply rumbling loudly.'

So I learnt what hypochondria was (although I think today we prefer the term "health anxiety" because after all, hypochondria is steeped in stigma, hence this chapter!). I felt so stupid as I "waste" someone's time with an "imagined" illness.

God, I'm such a drama queen. How much have I cost the NHS this time?

But I did have an illness that needed treating. I did have a legitimate reason to seek help. It just wasn't the illness I thought I was seeking help for. However, as a non-professional, surely it wasn't my responsibility to diagnose myself with Generalised Anxiety Disorder?

My other panic attacks during the 90s weren't quite as serious as the first one. They made me incredibly anxious, obviously, and they made me breathe heavily and feel faint, but I don't recall losing my vision again or having to grab onto railings. Other than the stress-induced occasional nosebleed that would occur after a row with a boyfriend or rushing to catch a bus, I think I pretty much covered up my anxiety.

Often, discovering a lump or rash would set me off. However, as things progressed, I would find myself feeling uncomfortable watching TV or lying in bed, as I would be conscious of my heartbeat. Being still was scarier than rushing for a bus. At least then I had a reason to feel my heart racing.

I must have a genetic heart problem.

I was acutely aware of all bodily sensations. Not in a nice, relaxing, mindfulness kind of way though. I was on the lookout for something that might go horribly wrong. At one time, after transient obsessions with lumps and rashes and heartbeats, I became obsessed with my throat. It felt like it was closing up. I was terrified that I might stop breathing. I could feel the edges of my throat and they were closing in, tighter and tighter.

My mum tried reflexology on me, but even that didn't help me relax. I was lying on a comfy bed, having a foot rub, and all I could think about was the tightening, tightening, tightening of my blasted throat. I felt like I had a lump in my throat for a week solid. I felt it from the moment I woke to the moment I fell asleep. It was like that feeling when you need to cry and you have to hold it in while at the same time having a bit of food or a tablet stuck in your throat. I was convinced that some unexplained, freak medical condition was about to take me to my inevitable early grave. Spontaneous strangulation. I'd never heard of it before, but I was sure I could be the first.

So, after crying down the phone at the receptionist and being given an emergency appointment, I went to see my GP. And I told him that my throat was closing up.

I think my records must have shown a certain pattern of behaviour, because he didn't ask to look at my throat. He knew the problem was borne of my brain.

Medical notes:

22/02/00 – Panic attacks since age 16. Sweats, palpitations etc. often due to worries re health. Self-confessed hypochondriac.

04/04/01 – Talk about hypochondria, anxious, worries, long chat.

28/06/01 – Feels slight swelling in throat with hot drinks.

04/07/01 – Anxiety ++ (I believe that means very anxious) – esp. re throat. Refer Angela.

Angela is the counsellor. I turned down the offer of beta blockers (I was scared of tablets). And I cried when the offer to talk to somebody came up. It felt like such a huge relief. I was going to front this stuff up. Angela was going to help me do it.

The referral letter stated:

Dear Angela

Problem – Anxiety

This 23-year-old woman is very frustrated and distressed by her feelings of anxiety, which are beginning to threaten her ability to cope with her job and are affecting her relationships. She says she has always been very anxious. Many years ago had one full-blown panic attack and is petrified of it reoccurring, especially when she is at work. She worries a great deal about minor physical symptoms and is unable to take the pill for fear of thrombosis. She is currently particularly worried about sensations in her throat. She is very clear about not wanting medication, but is desperate to gain control over her constant anxiety.

It's interesting that, on that day, I didn't realise the impact of the other panic attacks – the ones I must have thought were minor, the ones that were more constant. And what was also interesting was the fact that I was particularly worried about having a panic attack in front of people at work. I didn't know how to articulate it. And my boss didn't know how to manage it. Yes, I could go for counselling, as long as I wasn't gone too long. Yes, I could nip out at lunchtime for air, but as long as I didn't take too long.

We just didn't talk about it back then. It felt shameful, weak. In fact, it just felt ridiculous.

However, identifying the problem as anxiety didn't stop me turning up for my counselling sessions and complaining of my tight throat. My counsellor would send me to the bathroom and suggest I look in the mirror, open my mouth and see if my throat had actually closed up at all. Of course it hadn't.

More medical notes:

13/07/01 – Advice re rash on arm

13/07/01 – A&E – viral rash

So, this rash. This was the A&E trip for suspected "meningitis" – the Tesco rash event I mentioned before. It was a Friday night and I was happily doing the food shopping in Tesco, looking forward to having a pizza and watching *Friends*, when I noticed a teeny tiny rash on my arm, a tiny cluster of blood spots. They were tiny, pinprick sized marks. I rushed to the cashier, paid for the shopping, and drove straight to the walk-in centre.

The GP took my temperature, looked at the rash, basically checked me over and said it was highly unlikely that there was anything wrong with me, given the fact that I had no headache, fever, etc. However, he *did* say, 'That does look like the meningitis rash, so perhaps I should refer you to A&E just to be safe.'

Oh. My. God. I might be right this time.

I rushed to A&E, where I spent the remainder of my Friday night, my frozen pizza defrosting in the back of my Toyota Corolla which was parked in the most expensive hospital car park. And, to top it off, I was missing the return of Janice "Oh. My. God" Litman in that night's episode of *Friends*.

Why? Because I was left waiting for life-saving treatment until after the pubs chucked out.

When I was finally seen, the doctor was furious. Not with me – with the walk-in clinic GP. Apparently, there was no way on Earth that I could have meningitis. I had simply scratched myself and caused a slight bruising to my forearm.

Although they weren't directing their anger at me, I have to admit I felt ridiculous (I'm acutely aware of how often I am using this word). I felt like it was all my fault. However, my relief that that I wasn't about to die in Hull's A&E on a Friday night kind of outshone the ridiculousness of the situation. Thank God I wasn't going to die.

Perhaps it was the fact that it was Friday the 13th that subconsciously set me off? Whatever it was, it totally ruined the start to my weekend. My frozen pizza was soggy, my wine was lukewarm and my brain was mashed.

All of these instances involved some kind of bodily function or physical feeling, so I always thought I had a bladder problem or a stomach upset. It all linked to physical health and it all became confused because it would start through panic, anxiety or excitability, then immediately transform into a physical sensation. And I would then believe that the physical sensation was the actual problem, rather than the symptom of the actual problem.

It was nice being able to add that to the already turbulent mix of adolescence, periods, and heartbreak. Thanks, brain!

So, what does this prove? Well, nobody is immune to physical illness, that's for sure. But it's pretty reassuring when I look at some of my physical symptoms that I was convinced were the beginnings of a sinister illness. I can now see that they were, in fact, either caused by trying to carry a heavy pot of rhododendrons from one end of the garden to the other (thumb twitch / muscle strain) or the result of a poorly mind.

I'm not underestimating the effect that mental health can have physically. But the reason I can relax is because when I look at my

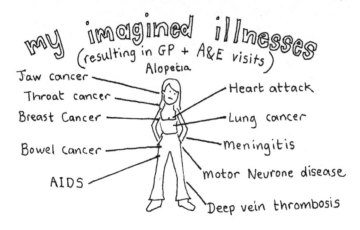

diagrams, it's clear that all of those "degenerative diseases" were, in fact, something else. Something not to get so wound up about.

Ah, but hang on a minute – my illness actually does most of the winding up itself, and it's not easily treated with a pill. So perhaps it is something to get wound up about?

The more your mind is drawn into the strong, suffocating arms of health anxiety, the worse the symptoms get. It's inevitable. It's a cycle that needs to be broken.

But it doesn't make me a 'wussy hypochondriac'.

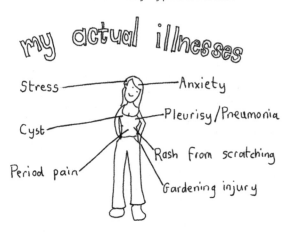

There is one illness on those diagrams that was pretty painful: pleurisy caused by pneumonia. I was a wreck when I didn't know what it was. But as soon as the x-ray results came back and I knew what I was dealing with, I rose to the challenge.

My 17-year-old pneumonia-riddled pleuritic lungs did not stop me donning high heels and a 90s shift dress from Bay Trading Co., hitting the Blue Lamp pub and snogging my ill-suited, long-haired, overly friendly teenage boyfriend. Sadly.

It's the unknown I couldn't deal with – not the diagnosis, not the pain and not the 90-Marlboro Red-a-day style hack. It was the fear of what I could have that bothered me so much.

What if it's a rare, one-in-a-million, progressive disease that causes your lungs to explode out of your chest and makes you spontaneously combust?

Oh, it's pneumonia. Cool. I'll go clubbing.

(Sorry Mum, I realise that meant an extra week of phlegmy convalescing on the sofa.)

So anxiety, and health anxiety in particular, doesn't make me weak. I'm not unable to deal with pain and illnesses. I'm just scared of the unknown. And that's another matter entirely.

People with health anxiety shouldn't feel guilty for breaking down at the GP surgery with a lump or a bump. Sometimes the root cause of certain symptoms is cancer, an infection or a cyst. But sometimes it's anxiety. The lump (which turned out to be a cyst) wasn't my only symptom. My symptoms also involved tears, shaking, feeling sick and tension – because anxiety is a real illness.

So, we should all stop feeling so ashamed, so guilty, so ridiculous. But Jesus, it's some crazy head shit that's going on. Anxiety that makes you rock back and forth and go to A&E and pace and think you're dying and see terrible images in your mind.

So to get over the idea that I was dying of a fatal disease, I had to admit that I was one hell of a psycho bitch.

CHAPTER 3

Stereotype: The Psycho Bitch

REALITY: THE 1 IN 4

You can often find me in town, shaking like a leaf, muttering to myself and pushing 18 cats in a pram.

That, of course, is a big fat lie. And another big fat stereotype.

If you bumped into me while I was shopping in town tomorrow, you wouldn't even notice me. Sadly, I'm just not that interesting.

We do talk more openly about mental health now, but if we're all really honest, perhaps we're still a tad frightened of it. Do we still conjure up, in our minds, stereotypical images of mentally ill people, of those who appear to have an edge to their madness?

If you saw a photo of me, you wouldn't think, *she has a mental illness*. I do not have PRONE TO PANIC stamped on my forehead. I am relatively normal, whatever that means. But sometimes, my illness makes me do some pretty 'out there' things, just like some of my physical illnesses do.

You might see me rocking back and forth, moaning, gripping my knees tightly to my chest and gritting my teeth. That would be my period pain.

You might see me slowly wobbling to the car outside the shop, looking a bit spaced out and unsteady. That will be my thyroxine levels dropping.

You might see me drifting in and out of consciousness thanks to a codeine intake, spluttering and coughing all over my duvet which I haven't washed for three days. That would be my pneumonia and pleurisy.

And you might see me pacing my front room quietly, chanting 'Be okay, be okay, be okay ...' to myself, tears streaming down my face while I furiously wring my hands. That would be my anxiety.

So you see, admitting I have a mental health condition does not mean I'm a crazy person. But illnesses – both mental and physical – can have some seemingly crazy-looking symptoms and behaviours attached to them. And anxiety and panic is not excused from this.

Crazy-looking behaviours and symptoms are borne of depression, schizophrenia, period pain, hypothyroidism, anxiety, pneumonia, stomach bugs, panic, and the common cold. Yes, seriously – the common cold. If you weren't full of cold, would you usually talk in that strange voice and cough green phlegm all over your bed? And what about the common stomach upset? Would you usually roll around under the duvet moaning and groaning, perhaps doing the *absolute unthinkable*?

Oh come on, shitting yourself isn't confined to crazy people, you know!

So this proves that mental illness isn't responsible for *all* of these seemingly anti-social, "embarrassingly cringey" behaviours and symptoms. We are much more likely to excuse them if they are borne of a physical problem, though.

So now I've got that off my chest, and we know that mental illness is not the only thing that can make you look crazy, I can say that yes, anxiety can have pretty full-on symptoms. It can be a pretty full-on mental illness.

Part of the stress of panic is wondering if you're crazy. *My head created all this stress and from what? From nothing.*

This is another burden that I don't need, on top of everything else. It's funny, I can write on the subject of mental health, volunteer for Time to Change, and campaign against stigma. But still when my symptoms return I think, *I bet they never knew I was this crazy though! Perhaps I'm too unhinged, too emotional, too crazy to speak out in public?*

But mental illness affects 1 in 4 people. It's not exactly rare!

Why do we feel guilty for what our minds do? If someone has diabetes, do we criticise their diet? If someone gets gout do we have a pop at their "overindulgence"? Sometimes – but not so much. Not as much as we do it to ourselves with mental illness. But it's just another part of the body – and in fact, the brain is made of physical matter.

So why do we treat mental illness with such disdain, especially when we have first-hand experience and evidence of how bloody cruel it can be? We're essentially treating *ourselves* with disdain.

I always felt there was something dark and scary about mental illness. Growing up, I knew many people who lived with mental health issues, but I can't pretend I understood them at the time. And I didn't relate my experience of panic and anxiety in any way to depression, schizophrenia, addiction or other illnesses that I saw friends dealing with. Not that they are necessarily comparable, it's just that the problems all stem from the same place. I was imposing stigma on myself and other people.

Thinking back to the 90s, when I was making the difficult transition into adulthood, I really wasn't so understanding of mental illness. I remember saying to a friend, 'What on Earth are you depressed about? We're sitting in front of the fire, drinking wine. Life is good.' I felt frustrated that he wouldn't just "snap out" of his low mood. I went to bed that night and left him on the sofa. The next morning I got up to find he had vanished – along with a whole bottle of Smirnoff that had been patiently waiting in the kitchen cupboard for the next Friday night out. I was angry at him. On some level, I think I thought his addiction to alcohol was a choice.

I never would have believed my panic attack was a choice though.

I also remember angrily informing another friend, who had appeared at our back door in the middle of the night, that he had scared my housemates, and so I wasn't going to invite him in. He was having some issues and wanted a place to stay that night. Sadly, I will never have the opportunity to invite him in, or indeed speak to him, again. His mental illness got the better of him after many years of suffering and he took his own life. He was suffering from something that many of us didn't understand.

In these situations, my friends were not simply whinging about nothing or acting in a scary way to get attention. They were ill.

Although I didn't realise it at the time, I was *starting* to consume media that challenged stereotypes. Arnold Schwarzenegger was a terminator and a kindergarten teacher in Hollywood films. And Madonna made it very clear that she was no longer a virgin (okay, so by the 90s I knew Madonna's 'Like a Virgin' wasn't literally trying to tell us she was a bona fide virgin. But I was an innocent child in the 80s and I didn't understand that).

Movies like *Home Alone* taught us all that the scary man with the snow shovel who lived down the road wasn't really a bad man, but a lonely old neighbour who missed his family. We were taught to look beyond the surface. And, although it was penned many years earlier by Harper Lee, having *To Kill a Mockingbird* on my English GCSE reading list encouraged me to entertain the idea that the local recluse might actually be a nice guy. Of course I'm talking about Boo Radley here: another feared character who reaches out for friendship and, towards the end of the book, saves the children's lives in a heroic act.

But as young teens, we were obsessed with our interesting neighbours from the local "nut house" – as we so affectionately referred to the supported accommodation in our village.

Back then we thought the residents of said accommodation were all mad. They were people living with mental health issues or learning disabilities or illnesses like dementia. They were proper "crazy". Weird. Mad. Nut jobs.

I'm not proud of this.

Cedar Grange, the village "nut house", was a scary old building which stood behind the bus stop where I had my first ever awkward snog.

I guess it didn't help that Cedar Grange was a big, old, Victorian building with a long, dark driveway surrounded by big trees. Steps up to a huge arched doorway – set within a central tower with a pointed roof – and a dark attic window gave it a kind of *Hammer House of Horror* feel. Combine that with a naïve, teenage view of the residents and games of truth or dare and you have the makings of *The Village Witch Project*.

The village kids would dare each other to run into the gardens and around the house. Our hearts would race as we took on the challenge. It was scary. We thought the residents were dangerous. Or just really, really weird.

One resident made the mistake of telling us that he was going to marry his cat. Today, as the proud owner of three furry felines, I find that rather sweet. Here was somebody who probably didn't have many friends, so he obviously found comfort in spending time with his pet cat. But that's not how we saw it back then. Our cries of 'I'm gonna kill that cat!' must have made our parents proud. They had nurtured such loving, accepting, and tolerant children ... but I guess we weren't much different from any other kids in the 90s.

One girl we knew, Helen, lived around the corner from Cedar Grange. She was always scared of it too. One Halloween, Helen and her friends dared each other to play trick or treat there. They nervously crept up the driveway, trying to push each other to the front, then the unlucky soul who ended up at the front was forced to ring the doorbell. There was no turning back now!

So what happened? Were they greeted by the Addams family? Did Norman Bates try to slash them with a dagger? Was Hannibal Lecter kept in a glass cage like some kind of grotesque Damien Hirst art exhibit?

Nope.

One of the staff answered the door and invited the nervy mob in. And they had a bloody riot! They met the staff and the residents, most of whom had learning disabilities. And we'd been calling them mad!

One resident with Down syndrome joined in with the group's Halloween antics, threw a tea towel over his head and shouted 'boo!' at the now chilled out and happy friends. Helen said that was the day that her entire view of Cedar Grange changed. It's ironic, really, that it was Halloween night when she realised something she had always been afraid of wasn't actually scary in any way, shape or form.

We should *never* have told that guy from Cedar Grange that we were going to kill his cat! We should have listened to Harper Lee and Macaulay Culkin.

But mental health, in my opinion, still mainly suffered from dangerous representations in the media. The occasional stigma-busting stories were great, but they were still fighting against a reinforced image constantly peddled to us through TV, films, books and the like.

Disclaimer – this is not based on academic study, so there may well have been a fairly decent proportion of positive representations, but this is what stands out in my memory: the mainstream stuff that I watched in the 90s. That's the stuff we chose to consume.

Lesson: a girl with borderline personality disorder (BPD) will kill your dog, sleep with your boyfriend and steal your identity. Film: *Single White Female*. I was 14 when this film came out. I was about to have what I *thought* was my first panic attack. I had no understanding of mental illness and I hadn't even heard of borderline personality disorder. This bitch was just a "psycho".

The synopsis in my own words: Bridget Fonda advertises for a single white female (I know!) and Jennifer Jason Leigh rocks up, appearing to be sweet and shy (and donning endearing floral 90s fashion – think of Blossom from the US teatime show of the same name) but in fact she's hiding a "deadly secret". That secret, it turns out (and according to Wikipedia), is borderline personality disorder. And apparently this makes Jennifer Jason Leigh's character a crazed killer. Struggling with her own identity, she adopts the identity of her housemate, Fonda, and gradually becomes dangerously ingrained in her life. Then her stiletto heel becomes dangerously ingrained in the boyfriend's eye. Well, fatally ingrained actually. This chick had some shit going on!

But this wasn't the first time we'd come across BPD in a movie, was it? We'd already seen Glenn Close in the film *Fatal Attraction* back in the 80s. So now we have a dead bunny *and* a dead doggie on our hands!

Surely anyone with a diagnosis of BPD must not be allowed within five miles of any furry pets and must be immediately reported to the RSPCA. Or so it would seem ...

Can you imagine if you were labelled with BPD in the 80s and 90s? Might all of this have impacted on your recovery? I don't see how it couldn't have. But even today, where are our heroes with the BPD diagnosis?

"Bunny boiler" became the throwaway label we gave to "crazy" women who "stalked" their men. I admit, I used it on many occasions. And I'm not saying that *Fatal Attraction* and *Single White Female* are badly made films, it's just, on balance ... well, was there any balance?

Another illness we learnt about through Hollywood was obsessive compulsive personality disorder. If your husband places all the tins of baked beans and vegetable soup in a neat row and lines your bath towels up symmetrically, you're gonna have to get out quick, fake your own death and always, always keep one eye open.

I'm talking about 90s film *Sleeping with the Enemy*. Patrick Bergin portrayed domestic violence very well. He portrayed obsessive compulsive personality disorder less so (not a critique of the performance, of course), because – until David Beckham spoke out years later about a similar illness – thanks to films like this we were led to believe that lining up tins was a sure sign of pure evil. No equilibrium.

Remember at the end of the film when Patrick broke in to Julia Roberts' new house and he'd been rearranging her cupboards? And that dark and terrifying soundtrack that went with it? Yep. Stay away from these crazed cupboard organisers.

They kill too! For me, that scene represents as much impending doom as the Red Rum tricycle scene in *The Shining*.

Even if we didn't know what the specific diagnosis was for a character's mental illness, seeing its symptoms associated with violent behaviours and terrifying possibilities created a negative connection between mental illness and violence. We needed to see people experiencing hallucinations and creating great works of art; we needed to see people with BPD as loving family members; we needed to see people with depression on the dance floor, having a laugh. In fact, we just needed to see normal life. We needed more balance.

I am quite sure there were other films that were more positive in their portrayals, but the problem is that they don't stand out in my memory. And that makes me think that they didn't help shape my views on mental illness growing up. All the ones that spring to mind are thrillers or horrors that featured victimised people at the hands of scary monsters with mental illnesses. There were movies based in haunted asylums, where the ghosts of "crazed" former patients would come back to wreak their revenge on some teenage group and their makeshift Ouija board. Why would anyone want to seek help if it ultimately meant being chained up in a Victorian asylum, and losing yourself to violence and terror?

The only film that stands out to me from my younger years – as one that sensitively tackled mental illness – is *Dead Poets Society*, which explored the issues of depression and suicide. I remember one of my GCSE school friends breaking down in tears when we watched it in class. For a change, we were not sniggering at "crazy" people. Instead we, a bunch of irritable egotistical teenagers, were genuinely touched by this movie. It's a tragic film, and even more so today in light of Robin Williams' tragic suicide. But I'm not sure the fact that mental illness is something that could affect anyone ever really sunk in. It still felt like someone else's problem.

Dead Poets Society actually showed the human side of mental illness, not the sensational stereotype. It portrayed somebody who was struggling due to pressures and illness. I'm not sure we could fault the treatment in that movie – but debate me if you think I'm wrong. I could be.

I have read articles – one from only a few years ago on the Time to Change website, quoting findings from a report by psychiatrist and film expert Dr Peter Byrne – that say movies are more stigmatising than ever. It's such a shame. I guess the lack of understanding and medical advances from many years ago didn't help matters. I once read a book by Catharine Arnold about Bedlam – the Victorian hospital, or "mental asylum" as it was known at the time. It is the world's oldest psychiatric hospital, and the book explores early explanations around mental illness – including the idea of demonic possession. There was even a 1940s horror film starring Boris Karloff called Bedlam. With endless tales of possession and lunacy, it was bound to be a stage for horror movies. Many years before that film came out, it was actually a popular pastime to gawp at Bedlam's inpatients. It was a kind of day trip for the curious.

Mental illness has often proved popular as entertainment. There's no bloody wonder we spent our spare time hanging out around the local Cedar Grange home waiting for something spooky to happen.

If an issue wasn't discussed openly, it would appear to be dark and sinister. I'm not surprised, because I guess it just wouldn't bring in the box office sales if a film about mental illness represented a successful, nice and "normal" person. Would it?

I mean, they could make sufferers look like successful people, perhaps – like in the films *American Psycho* and *The Wolf of Wall Street*. But nice and "normal" those characters are not.

And where does the psychopath fit in the world of mental health? Is it a mental illness or is it something else? I'm definitely not qualified to debate that one! So moving swiftly on …

I don't know about anyone else, but I quite liked the recent portrayals of mental illness in the most addictive of US dramas (in my opinion), *Homeland*. Me and my other half were absolutely glued to the story. Yes, it did portray its protagonist, Carrie, experiencing terrifying and dark symptoms of bipolar disorder, but it also challenged stigma. Even though she was a talented CIA agent, Carrie's theories were often dismissed as madness due to her diagnosis and she ended up being hospitalised. But eventually her theories were proven to be spot on. I think that goes a long way to show that mental illness, while it does cause distressing symptoms, does not affect somebody's entire personality or intelligence – despite what is often portrayed.

In fact, *Homeland* highlighted some of the positives that can be borne of having an illness like bipolar disorder. Carrie was clearly ill, but she was cracking the investigations when she was in a manic phase, working late into the night. I'm not suggesting this is healthy. But it's interesting to look at things differently. I think even Stephen Fry once said that while his illness sends him into dark depressions, it also gives him energy and creativity.

There are often different sides to it, though I wouldn't wish to say that these aspects of the condition are "good" for everyone. They can cause their own problems and create their own damage, of course.

Also in *Homeland*, we saw the character Peter struggling with post-traumatic stress disorder (PTSD). While his behaviours were extreme and concerning, his paranoia was based on actual events. Again, it just goes to show that the thoughts of someone experiencing delusions aren't necessarily always based on nonsense. I remember learning about that once, in a Futurelearn online course about caring for somebody with psychosis. Sometimes there is rhyme and reason behind seemingly "crazy" ideas, and that is why psychology is so interesting in this respect. Rationalising these thoughts can sometimes reconnect the person to reality. Not that I'm placed to do that of course – but I can see why psychologists have an important role to play in unravelling all of this.

The Girl on the Train had a similar message. It was one that showed us, the viewers, that we were wrong to think that the central character, Rachel, was so unreliable. She struggled with alcoholism. She was often intoxicated. Other train passengers were wary of her and moved their young children away from her. The police refused to believe her when she reported suspected crimes. But it didn't mean she wasn't right in her observations about her ex-husband and his reign of terror. It didn't mean everything she spoke of was nonsense. It didn't mean she was a "bunny boiler" (see what I did there? A double dose of stigma).

I do personally feel that in the main, TV and film today are a little more balanced today than in the 90s. People with mental illness are not simply scary or stupid or weak people. And *Homeland* was way more nail-biting than the 90s films I mentioned earlier (come on, season seven!) Mental health is tackled on mainstream TV too, with UK soaps like *EastEnders*, *Coronation Street* and *Emmerdale* exploring mental illness. Telling these stories through the nation's favourite soap characters creates empathy. It makes us realise that it can happen to anyone – it isn't restricted to a crack team of CIA agents fighting evil.

But at the end of the day, for people of my generation and those before us, we grew up with stereotypes. It's like the more you become exposed to something, the more immune you become and you start to lose sight of the facts. Mental illness stereotypes were as commonly consumed as Vesta ready meals and Findus crispy pancakes back then. None of it was good for us, but we knew no better. Celebrity chef Jamie Oliver wasn't rustling up a "pukka" salad with baked-not-fried sweet potato fries back then, it was the actual, unhealthy Pukka pie that was on offer.

And so how did all this stigma have an impact on me and my illness? Well, it meant I never understood my own mind. I also must have looked crazy to other people who didn't know any better either.

For me, anxiety was something that struck in all manner of seemingly illogical scenarios. Often publicly. I'm didn't think about how I looked to other people at the time, as my brain was far too focussed on not dying.

Maybe I did look crazy.

By the time I reached my late teens, I had developed a pretty irrational fear of public buses. Trains didn't scare me, planes didn't, even boats didn't. Cars were okay, although I hated that "new car" smell our Scirocco reeked of back in the 80s (I was always convinced it would make me chunder en route to Grandma's. Of course, it rarely did, but the thought of puking without a sink close by terrified me).

But buses have blighted many a memory and made me feel seriously crazy. I just felt an inexplicable fear for getting on them. Well, some of them.

For some reason, only the number 30 bus to North Hull Estate – where I lived with my boyfriend at the time – was acceptable. The number 30 bus wasn't as regular as the others, but it definitely gave me a much calmer experience. Why? I have no idea. I still can't rationalise it. But I was seriously scared of all other buses.

As I say, this fear didn't start till late on. The highlight of my school day as a 15-year-old was getting on the top deck of the bus to greet the Longcroft School lads with flour-and-water-bottle-fights. So why it suddenly became a vehicle of doom a few years later is beyond me.

In fact, I don't think I ever really truly imagined what would happen on the double deckers that dropped me off on Greenwood Avenue, as opposed to the mini buses that dropped me off on Endike Lane. Perhaps it was the fear of suddenly needing the loo, or being sick, or not being able to breathe. Maybe they were all mixed up in my mind somewhere, subconsciously.

I avoided those double deckers whenever I could.

Let's compare this behaviour to that caused by a physical illness. How about cystitis? I was only two stops from town one day when

I legged it, full pelt, off the bus and into the nearest pub to relieve my urgent need to pee (and this time, the urgent need to pee was created by a physical problem rather than a mental one). Same behaviour, different cause. The physical cause was perhaps rather more embarrassing, in hindsight – but notice I felt far less ashamed at the time.

Another scary and public environment for me was the theatre auditorium. During my early twenties, I worked for a great theatre company called Hull Truck Theatre. I got to watch tons of shows for free. The best were the dress rehearsal runs, where we wandered in, took a seat and put our feet up. There were only perhaps 10 or 12 of us during rehearsals, in an auditorium that held around 300 – so there was plenty of room to move about. Guest night was great fun too, after the show had finished.

My desk at Hull Truck Theatre, obviously some time before the digital revolution!

But it soon became apparent that taking whatever seat was spare during the busiest show of the run was a nightmare. If I didn't have an aisle seat when the show started, my face would drain of blood, goosebumps would appear on my skin, and I would hold tightly onto my seat, fidgeting constantly.

Will there be a quiet moment when I can dash out to the loo before the interval? I would think. Do I know anyone in this row? Will they mind moving to let me out? Is there a national critic sitting there who is going to write about it in The Guardian?

The next day's imaginary news article popped up in my head:

The show was top class, the acting superb, the direction slick, the script furiously firing out one hilarious gag after another. The viewing experience, however, was ruined as the Press Officer, who should really know better, interrupted proceedings by dashing out, cross-legged, to the loo every five minutes. Have Tena lady never found their way to Hull? Apparently not ...

Whenever I could I booked aisle seats, whether it cost me a ton more cash or not. Years later my husband Chris was performing in *The Pitmen Painters* at the National Theatre. It was a fabulous show written by Lee Hall of Billy Elliott fame. I'd seen it in every venue I could get to, even when it hit Broadway. This time, Chris had a free ticket for me. It was a great seat, he promised, trying to sell it to me. Central and close to the stage.

No. Bloody. Way. I paid £45 for a full-price seat on the end of a row instead, and left an obvious empty seat bang in the middle of an otherwise sold out theatre.

Mind you, panic could still strike me on the aisle seats. A lush night out with friends to see Gavin Webster – one of my favourite stand-up comedians from the North East – was completely ruined by fear. It wasn't the loo fear this time. It was the swallowing-my-saliva fear. I sat through laugh after laugh, trying to put on a brave face and giggle along with the crowd, but inside I was knotted up and incredibly tense.

I had a soft drink in the auditorium with me. I was driving that night. I got it into my head that I wasn't swallowing properly. Of course, the more you think about it, the more you have to do it, just to prove that you can, in fact, swallow like a normal human being. So I kept forcing myself to swallow over and over again, and the more I concentrated on it, the harder it became. I was thirsty, but taking a sip of lemonade felt like a life-threatening action. *What if I choke in the middle of the auditorium?* I panicked. *What if I ruin his legendary panda joke? What if I become one of his jokes?* (Which of course would never happen – I've only once seen Gavin Webster seriously heckle audience members, and that was when a bunch of pissed up coppers were making lewd comments about my friend's boobs. Twats. That was a heroic heckle.)

I would try to talk myself down from the panic, take a sip, really struggle to swallow and wind myself back up again in the process. It pretty much lasted the entire length of the show. As soon as I stood up to leave it disappeared. Typical.

So my big love of theatre was also a big bundle of fear, mostly concentrated around peeing myself and choking to death. Not normally what you'd associate with the arts (although you might find some stuff in this genre on Channel 4).

For the record, I will just state that no embarrassing urinary incidents ever actually occurred. Period. (Oh, *those* embarrassing incidents did sometimes occur though. Who wants to be seen buying humongous Super Plus Tampax in Sainsbury's? Not an issue for me these days of course – I've had plenty of practice and I know what happens if your protection level doesn't match your need! I'd much rather grab the Super Plus and a pack of Always Ultra, rather than risk walking around unwittingly with a bloodstained behind).

The pee fear did become another anxious obsession as I got older though. I would regularly leave buses, all-staff meetings and supermarket queues for fear of wetting myself in public.

And what's weird is that you associate certain situations or objects with the last time you felt the pee panic. During one of our all-staff meetings at work, I had to sit in the theatre foyer on one of those high wobbly bar stools – the type that are meant to look cool by making you wonder how they stay upright with no structural support. Well, they're proper wobbly. I had to sit on one of those – cross-legged and fidgety as we talked through the upcoming theatre season, and eventually had to leap off it and dash to the loos. I haven't been keen to sit on one of them again.

The supermarket queue. That's another scary public place to be. It's no longer a problem now (not now you can scan and shop and beat the queues – Christ, I speak like an advert), but I do remember abandoning my trolley mid-queue in Tesco one afternoon, as I was convinced I couldn't hold on. I dashed to the public loo, but not a lot happened. There really wasn't an issue, which I should have expected given I'd already been to the loo on my way in. Every time I went back to a supermarket queue after that I worried about it. I felt increasingly uncomfortable. Queuing in HMV or TopShop didn't bring it on though, only the supermarkets. It was an association – the scary supermarket slash. Or it could have been the fact that I found supermarket shopping dull, while bagging a new Sonic Youth CD or a tiny black dress for a night out in a cheesy club were far more exciting things to do.

Anyway, I went to see my GP. He asked if the unintentional urinary release that I feared so badly had ever actually happened.

'No,' I said.

And he seemed rather surprised that the more alcohol I consumed on a night out, the less often I felt the need to pee. Obviously it was my anxious mind, not my weak bladder, causing the sensation.

He prescribed some kind of drugs that increased my bladder volume anyway. He said I probably didn't need them because it sounded like anxiety, but of course I was more than happy to take them.

It seems strange to prescribe something like that when there was no obvious need. However, they may well have been a placebo.

None of this was fun. In fact, it was all incredibly embarrassing. What strange behaviour! People must have thought I was nuts, a psycho! After all, they'd been fed years of stigmatising media content!

The fact is, illness isn't meant to be a pleasant experience. But it doesn't make me crazy. I don't always have period pain, my thyroxine levels don't always drop and I don't always have anxiety attacks. I am not crazy. I am not terrified. I am not weak. But all of these illnesses can make me feel like it at times. The symptoms often seem a little crazy. But not me.

Could you spot anxiety in a line up?

A fake profile:

Name _____ Psycho bitch _____
Where you can
find me _____ In town, muttering to myself
Diagnosis _____ Weird. Mad. A nutjob. _____
Appearance _____ Crazy _____
Hobbies _____ Pushing 18 cats in a pram
My friends
describe me as _____ Emotional, dramatic, eccentric _____
The one thing I
can't live without _____ Drugs or alcohol _____

A real profile:

Name _____ Lucy _____
Where you can
find me _____ On twitter _____
Diagnosis _____ Generalised Anxiety Disorder
Appearance _____ Girl next door _____
Hobbies _____ Writing, running, gardening, cats
My friends
describe me as _____ Excitable – like a spaniel.
One full fat coke away from licking someone.
The one thing I
can't live without _____ Caffeine _____

I worked as hard as I could to cover up my "crazy" symptoms. Nobody needed to know why I was getting on a later bus. Nobody needed to know that I was wearing two panty liners under my bridesmaid dress for my friend's wedding "just in case". Nobody needed to know the real reason I often got off the bus early.

And with the help of alcohol, I would find it much easier to hide these unappealing symptoms, these weaknesses. Well, alcohol and then some ...

CHAPTER 4

Stereotype: The Party Addict

REALITY: THE LOST, ANXIOUS SOUL

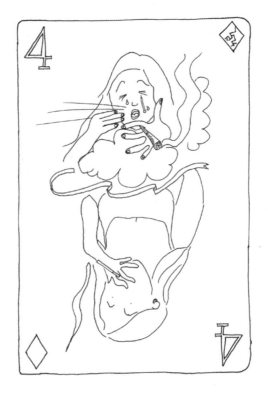

It's ridiculous, really, that for someone who was terrified of taking the contraceptive pill, the lure of chemical concoctions – the kind that spawned drugs tsars due to their tragically lethal consequences – was just too hard to resist.

I was never exactly overindulgent, and it was strictly weekends only. But for someone with anxiety, Sunday mornings were the absolute pits. And that was enough to wipe out a full week with anxious thoughts.

So where did the chemical romance – and my desire to be bad – begin?

1992. I was 14.

Are you there, God? It's me, Lucy.

I don't know how to ask you for this. I know it's wrong.

But please, can you give me some shaky ground?

Can something happen around here?

Life is so flat. Who will remember me like this?

Please make me hard-faced and interesting.

Amen.

The only A grade I got at GCSE was in Art. I loved it and I dreamt of being the next tortured soul to appear on the cover of *The Face* magazine.[3]

My idols were alternative punk / rock / arty girl band types including Courtney Love, Kim Deal, and Kristin Hersh. My own artwork mainly consisted of me designing new record sleeves for the bands I loved and creating dark images with "real" meaning and "depth" behind them. Generally, that meaning was entirely based on the fickle musings of a 14-year-old. So I guess my previous statement is debatable.

---

3 The trendy magazine I would leave lying around so people knew I was cool enough to read it. By "people", I mean my parents, who listened to Wet Wet Wet and Waylon Jennings.

I got myself a boyfriend – my first, with green hair, para boots and an inexplicable love of US punk band, The Dead Kennedys. My love of Prince and Roxette, therefore, was put firmly into retirement, along with my black choker and rubber platform shoes (if only I'd hung on to them – I'd make a fortune on eBay now they're back on trend). They were lost in the depths of a mahogany Stagg wardrobe that my parents donated to me when they upgraded their bedroom. (They shouldn't have bothered. After the refurb, my sister's friend sprayed the walls with Diamond White cider-scented vomit. That wasn't art. And puke wasn't punk. Well, not when it was sprayed on the walls of a new-build family home in a tiny village, anyway.)

My life was too comfortable. It was time to rip up my tights, go to gigs in spit-and-sawdust pubs and buy all my clothes from vintage shops. I often stank of mothballs but I swear I looked the part. (Debatable.)

Mind you, I was so straight-laced that my version of "grunge" was smoking a Marlboro Red at my bedroom window while wearing one glove so the tobacco smell wasn't detectable on my fingers. God forbid my mum caught me! In fact, even my green-haired para-booted boyfriend gave me a stern lecture when he found out I was occasionally swallowing the smoke of a cigarette in my pursuit of "inhaling properly". Shall we blame the candy cigarettes we had as kids? I'm guessing a large proportion of the kids who grew up munching on those things progressed onto the harder stuff.

During my teen years I lived in a picturesque little village, about three miles west of Beverley, a small town in East Yorkshire.

Cherry Burton was a fairly affluent village, which I guess is why the bus service was so shoddy – most people had at least two cars, so bus companies made very little money. For us kids who couldn't drive, however, we had to make do with entertaining ourselves within the confines of the village boundary. The village had a shop, a post office, a pub, a pond and a couple of bus stops. Think of UK soap *Emmerdale* before it dropped "Farm" from the title and got all sexy with dangerous liaisons, middle class farmers fayre shops and plane crashes.

So, with very little to go on, we looked to the village boys for entertainment. The ones a couple of years older were great fun for those flour-and-water-bottle fights on the school bus. That routine lasted a few weeks, but then we got a mention in assembly and a warning that we would be banned from all East Yorkshire buses if the behaviour continued. That was a concept we couldn't entertain – relying on our parents to escape village life. We reluctantly put a stop to the water fight fun. And I'm not sure we would have got away with taking more flour from the Home Economics classroom anyway – Miss almost had a meltdown when she found us hiding in the cupboard, playing with her beloved fabric. God knows what she'd have done if she caught us nicking off with flour and eggs. She was of a fairly nervous disposition.

We looked to the older village lads for something more interesting. We weren't able to actually hang out with them. They wouldn't have let us silly little school lasses, in our navy and white uniforms, ruin their scene. But still, we were in awe of them. We called them the "bench lads". They hung out by (you guessed it) the village bench (which was soon removed by the council) and the bus stop (which also got removed by the council). This was the early 90s.

I imagine the older locals thought the bench lads brought bad vibes to a village that prided itself on Santa Claus visiting the pond by boat each year, the local agricultural college and a strong Neighbourhood Watch society. Yep, thinking about it, the standard daily image of the boys' battered red Ford Fiesta parked up by the bench – with The Prodigy's 'Charley' pumping out of its stereo on a loop – never made it into the proud village newsletter.

Charley the cat was the poster-boy moggy for "stranger danger" in the 80s, thanks to the public information film of the same name. He and his young owner were later sampled on The Prodigy's big hit, again, of the same name. Rave culture reminded us of the things we should be frightened of. Charley says to always tell your mummy before you go off somewhere, after all!

There's no wonder my generation is fucked up and cynical. We were always being made to be frightened of life back then.

My friend walked past the bench lads one night. They were in the bus stop at the top of the village (they shouldn't have been – that was our hangout. But we were hardly going to attempt to boot them out). One of the lads, who looked like one half of Candy Flip,[4] was taking a leak at the bus stop while (apparently) saying 'Guys – I'm pissing blue and green!' This had to be the result of acid. LSD. God, these

4 A singing duo that covered the 'Strawberry Fields Forever' song in 1990.

guys were cool. We spent every single day at school discussing their hilarious antics as if we were mates with them. Part of the crowd, part of their scene.

Of course we weren't. We were busy doing chemistry theory while they were busy carrying out the chemistry experiments, completely unsupervised.

(Useless fact – "candy flip" is actually the slang term for dropping e (ecstasy) and LSD at the same time. Drug references in the music charts were pretty apparent in those days. One that particularly stands out is 'E's Are Good' by The Shaman. It had far more front than 'Golden Brown' by The Stranglers, but far less talent was involved in its creation.)

I longed to be different and unpredictable (like the village bench boys). In fact, that entire period of adolescence seemed to be based solely on inner conflict. Was I a rave fan or a grunge fan? Now *that* was a serious and torturous debate to have in my head! I had "Nirvana" written in biro on one side of my Memorex tape, and on the other, the not at all cheesy "Ratpack" was scrawled in felt pen (basically, that was some dodgy recording of an MC shouting a lot about ganja and love doves. I thought it made me cool to own it. Especially given that the tapes were passed down from Candy Flip guy to his younger brother and then to me).

In the end, however, I chose Nirvana.

Still, no amount of sun-in, cherry red lipstick, and white fishnets were going to change the fact that I wasn't really all that edgy. I always felt slightly uncomfortable turning up to school ten minutes late. My friends rejoiced in signing the late book with "aliens hijacked the bus," knowing it would piss the school office off. My signature, however, accompanied something less provocative, rather beige, and sincerely apologetic. *"Sorry – bus turned up late."*

Although I was one of the least rebellious among our group, I read everything I could about drugs. I had a real fascination with them.

I remember reading a book called *Dangerous Candy* by Raffaella Fletcher. It described the ups and downs of her relationship with heroin. The ups seemed to stand out more than the downs to me. And even the downs seemed endearingly edgy. I read it at least three times. She had been somewhere I hadn't – a curious, chemical-fuelled place. A place that would realise my dream of having a tortured soul.

Drew Barrymore was another star who had written about drug problems. She was super cool *and* she made it into the Courtney Love circle of wild-child fun and games.

So I made a realisation. You need some badness in your life to be somebody.

I was on a mission. I had the Regal cigarettes that I possibly wasn't inhaling properly and the buzz of sitting at my slightly older friend's flat with endless cups of syrupy black coffee. I smoked the ciggies (sort of) but I never bought them. That might have taken "bad" a step too far. If we ran out, we sometimes tried making a roll-up with dirty tab-ends and an envelope in the absence of Rizla papers. It tasted odd. I was terrified for days afterwards that I might have given myself lung disease. Thank God Google didn't exist back then.

I stared and stared at a 1993 cover of *The Face* magazine with Courtney Love on it. She had red lippy, peroxide hair, a heart pendant around her neck and seriously big, smudgy eyes. Oh, and a rumoured heroin addiction.

I used to fantasise about being at some sleazy party with Kurt and Courtney. There was a crisis because Kurt had taken a drug overdose and I was caught up in the drama. We were all in it together. The seedy, darkened glamour.

Why did I have to live in a village? I wanted Seattle.

So, I gave edgy a try. Well ... sort of.

Everyone knew the "secret" about the joke shop in town. The guy there served you liquid gold – or poppers. I don't remember too much about the effects of that stuff, other than it making everything turn yellow, making you laugh briefly but hard enough to nearly wee yourself, and leaving you with a banging headache.

Aloof? Me? A teenager's bedroom in the 90s.

I'm not sure this is what inspired 'Yellow' by Coldplay.

We tried dipping our ciggies in our little pot of liquid gold and inhaling them for a bigger "hit". I wasn't very good at biology – I hadn't considered that whether you inhale through your mouth or your nose it all goes to the same place. But it felt a bit naughtier.

So on to the next little experiment. We cranked "edgy" up a notch, with a few flakes of cannabis in a yoghurt. Meh.

I stayed out one night for this much anticipated illegal high, but when I didn't come home, my dad immediately assumed that my innocent boyfriend had taken advantage of me.

I'd become complacent. I used a plan I'd used before, carefully concocted between me and my best mate, saw us successfully fool our parents with fake telephone conversations about what we were going to do at each other's house that night. I told my mum that I was heading down the road to meet Cathryn, who was picking me up with her mum. Cathryn "unexpectedly" spotted me en route and told her mum she would jump out there to walk to my house. We slowly headed towards mine until her mum's car was out of sight, then turned on our heels and took a detour to my boyfriend's hippy shed where we stayed for the night.

I'd thought that I could pull it off again. But without my confident mate for back up this time, I had spectacularly failed.

So, after being found out, I tried to convince my dad that I had done something else, something possibly more forgivable in a father's eyes than staying at your boyfriend's house. I locked myself in the bathroom in fear and my dad shouted at me through the door.

Dad: 'Tell me the truth – where were you?'

Me: 'I was in town with Anna, drinking. Honest.'

Top tip – do not add on the word "honest", because it tells the person you're trying to convince that you are being, in fact, the opposite.

Dad: 'Okay Lucy. I'll call Anna's parents.'

Me: 'No! Don't do that! Please don't!'

Dad: 'Give me one good reason why I shouldn't.'

Me: 'Because ... I wasn't with Anna.'

The truth was, I spent the night in my boyfriend's hippy shed, listening to Nirvana and Senseless Things, burning incense and eating a tasteless yoghurt with black lumps in it. There was no funny business involved, just the illegal yoghurt. I'm not sure if it had any effect though. I said I could hear a helicopter that apparently wasn't there. Ooh ... the illegal yoghurt must have done something!

I remember when, aged five, I said I could hear Santa's sleigh bells in the sky. They weren't there either – and I'm pretty sure the Petit Filous I ate then contained no illegal ingredients (besides, the five-year-old me hated yoghurts and fruit juices with lumps in). So I wonder whether I actually had cannabis with my boyfriend after all. You can talk yourself into all sorts when you're young and excited.

I once believed Mighty Mouse was flying around my living room. I was about six. Turned out it was my mum fooling me.

So anyway, back to my family bathroom lock-in. I 'fessed up. I unlocked the bathroom door, came out of hiding and stopped in my room for the day. I was unhappy at being caught, but happy about breaking bad. (Is that an anachronism?) Maybe I did have the potential to make it into *The Face* one day?

Meanwhile my sister was behaving badly and getting shit loads of grief for it. I remember her kicking off one day and my mum shouting 'Jesus, you sound like you're on drugs!'

My sister retorted, '*I'm* not the one on drugs. Ask your other precious daughter.'

My mother, given her catastrophising and terrified reaction (and you wonder where I got it from!) must have pictured my episode with an illegal pot of Petit Filous as me having a full-blown heroin addiction. Still, she appreciated my honesty when I explained things, so it calmed down relatively quickly. That didn't stop her, weeks later, storming into my room when she heard me telling my sister to "sniff this", though. She looked massively relieved, albeit slightly red-faced, when she was confronted with her two teenage daughters sniffing the Body Shop's Dewberry oil rather than a bag of glue.

I moved out, aged 17, to some dodgy flat in Hull while still studying for my A Levels. I ditched the bleached jeans and second hand cardies, squeezed my blue painted toe nails into a cheap pair of heels, and hit the clubs on a regular basis. It wasn't glam.

By this point, I had broken up with green-haired para-booted boyfriend. Heart. Broken. People tell you that the first time is the worst – it's really not. It's just a new and unexpected overload of feelings. You realise you were never actually going to get married aged 18 anyway and the heartbreak is very quickly fixed by a snog with a long-haired teenage lothario at a party.

Big mistake.

Seeing in the millennium a little worse for wear.

Given how I was still pretty scared of people and newly single, it was a daunting experience. Lambrini helped me and my friends enormously though – not least because we could buy a 150cl bottle for just a couple of quid and our tastebuds hadn't matured enough to take the next step in wine appreciation (Chardonnay). Lambrini was like drinking a sweet and sugary fizzy drink. But surely it's a step forward from Diamond White cider and Mad Dog 20/20 in terms of sophistication?

Being skint all the time, we'd down our fizzy Lambrini (one bottle each) before hitting a club in our full-length chiffon and lycra dresses (they were about as sophisticated as our choice of beverage). While the dancefloor gave me a sense of comfort (given the fact you didn't have to converse with anyone), the chillout room, bizarrely, was a place of heightened anxiety for me. If I wasn't gouching out off a pill I was forced to make conversation. And I still had no idea how to do that. *Perhaps if I just loll my head back and slap an inane smile on my face, people will just think I'm high and leave me alone?*

I did venture into the world of amphetamines and psychoactive drugs after a while. There must have been a reason why those MCs kept banging on about this stuff. But even with all that fake energy, combined with a super-high adrenaline boost from my anxiety, I was a rubbish clubber.

It seemed that no matter what illicit drugs my housemate introduced me to, I was always ready to fall asleep before anyone else (although I often made it through to that awful moment when daylight breaks through your cheap, badly hung curtains. A terrible time for an anxiety sufferer who had become too sensitive to stomach even a black coffee, yet decided to venture into a new world of drug taking regardless). I would often spend a ridiculous amount of time wondering if this was going to be the drug that would kill me. Wha if I had a bad reaction? What if my heart stopped? What if my circulation failed?

But still, I'd done something cool!

Having had very little sleep, I'd trundle back to my mum's on a Saturday afternoon, complaining about a strange, swollen ridge that had appeared in the roof of my mouth due to my being dehydrated as hell. 'Oh my god, Mum, I'm so dehydrated, I can't even eat a chocolate biscuit. The roof of my mouth is swollen and I can't swallow my food properly. What is wrong with me?!'

When you're that age you think you know it all. I thought my new lifestyle meant that my mum could never understand me. Often I would think, *I know something you don't know and wouldn't understand, because I've entered a world you couldn't dare to imagine.*

Of course, as a 39-year-old step-parent, I now know that my own parents were probably not as green as I thought they were.

So anyway, with my new and (in)significant experience with party drugs (probably just enough white powder to get a small hamster running on its wheel), I had taken hold of this grownup lifestyle and I was running with it.

At college, I got a D in Art, an E in English, and an E in Law. I had a handle on life, just not the right kind. And they were bloody right about A Levels – they are the hardest exams you'll ever take, mainly because the majority of people who sit them are busy ditching their fake ID for the real deal. And that is guaranteed to get them served, sozzled, and shit-faced. It's kind of hard to study in that state, never mind sit through a formal exam. Hence the E in Law – I sat that exam having emerged from my friend's house at 5am with extreme double vision and a restless stomach. I was not unique. A lot of us were discovering and exploiting our legal entitlements. It's a seriously difficult age!

Remember the bench lads from the village? Well, during a trip back home one Christmas I ended up snogging Candy Flip guy. We hung out at his dad's house with my sister, who was seeing his brother (keep up – small village life can lead to these too-close-for-comfort circumstances). I was trying to impress Candy Flip guy by having a puff on the joint that was being passed around.

Three minutes later I was desperately trying to curb the ensuing nausea by eating a slice of dry bread. Then I passed out, hugging the toilet.

Hungover at my place of solace (aka Mum's house).

Wet and muddy at Glastonbury 98.

I have a vague memory of people having to step over me when they needed to pee.

After this encounter with Candy Flip guy, we ended up spending five years together, on and off. He wasn't singing 'Strawberry Fields Forever' and pissing rainbows anymore. He was a labourer who worked hard, drank a bit too much Oranjeboom lager (eight for a fiver in the local off-licence), had questionable political arguments, and was not to be trusted with the girls. It wasn't the psychedelic dream I had imagined, although he did introduce me to ecstasy while watching *Watership Down* one Friday night. That was an experience. Big Wig's doomed fate made my heart pound out my chest and I begged him to run to safety.

'Run, Big Wig! RUUUUUNNNNN!'

Was it a proper good "e" or a joint that exposed my passion for the lives of cartoon rabbits? I guess I'll never know ... after all, I still can't watch any David Attenborough wildlife programmes without coming close to a panic attack, so it's a real possibility that I didn't actually get high that night.

Thinking about it, I really was gullible then. Candy Flip Guy told me one night, as we were sitting in the local pub, that the two men sitting nearby were a drug dealer and a hitman. I totally bought it. Mind you, given the kick I got under the table when I confidently informed one of the alleged "gangsters" that he had the dress sense of Alan Partridge, perhaps there was something in it. In fact, I'm sure I recall one of them making it into the Hull Daily Mail court files …

So, was that an authentic "e" and a hitman, or a Sherbert Dib Dab and a criminology student? Who knows?

Looking back, those little substances I was using to complement my cheap Lambrini didn't really do me much good at all. Combine everything at once and you've got a really interesting mood. They totally ruined my Glastonbury experience in 1998. Along with the relentless rain and knee-high mud, half a little pill made me feel completely overwhelmed, just as indie band Primal Scream took to the stage. The panic set in. Woah – my head was swimming, my chest felt odd and the field I was standing in suddenly seemed ten times bigger than it was. I listened to the rest of their act from the confines of our tiny tent that, by that point, was flooded with rainwater and mud. The seasoned Candy Flip guy wasn't that impressed with his early night.

A while later, I broke up with Candy Flip guy (for about the eighth time, although not the last). Feeling devastated and on edge, I went out on a night out with a friend. Not long past midnight, they dropped me off at my parent's big empty house, having literally just inhaled some dirty white powder. Speed again. Cheap and nasty. The Fray Bentos of illegal substances.

With no Netflix or social media in existence, I struggled to find anything to stop my brain whirring at a thousand miles an hour. And given it was now 1am, there wasn't even *Brookside*, *A Question of Sport*, *Murder Most Horrid* or *You've Been Framed* to distract me. Damn my friends. That was not drug-taking etiquette. You don't put your body and brain into overdrive then leave each other to ponder the meaning of life alone at high speed. So I sat and paced and sat and paced in my room for what felt like an eternity.

Illegal substances have made me:

- Miss two hair appointments
- Inadvertently summon the police to my front door (I was screaming. Loudly.)
- Miss the best acts at Glastonbury
- Wander alone down a disused railway track (a demanding millennium reveller ripped my top, saying he wanted a kiss NOW!)
- Miss a friend's wedding reception
- Get a speeding ticket after panicking behind the wheel
- Spend a morning with my feet in a basin of warm water because I thought my circulation had gone
- Burst into tears at a party
- Burst into tears in front of the police while they held my mate on the ground for forcibly buying booze before 11am
- Throw a delicious pizza in the bin because I thought I was having a heart attack
- Black out, puke up, hyperventilate, sweat like a pig, and dance like a zombie on high speed

IT'S JUST NOT THAT COOL!

But there were negative legal substances too. I'm not talking about the (il)legal highs of today. The only "legal highs" we had back then were tantamount to smoking PG Tips. And no, this one was not a legal high you would buy from the dodgy alternative fetish shop based in a back-street basement complete with whips and a dentist's chair (how many Hull peeps remember Function One?) This substance could be bought in branded cans from the paper shop. I'm talking about taurine. Because a new soft drink was going to give us all wings ...

The first time I drank Red Bull was in Crete with a good friend.

I drank it all night with vodka. The next day, I frantically followed my friend, who had a very real and obvious eye infection, to the emergency health centre. I told them I was having palpitations and was worried about my heart. Panic, again. But that didn't stop me adopting the drink that gives you wings when I returned home to our regular haunt Buzz Bar, Hull's finest city centre offering in the pre-City of Culture days. Sophistication at its best. Ahem.

It seems so obvious now that if you suffer from anxiety then Red Bull, speed, black sugary coffee, nicotine, and alcohol are not especially suitable for you. Well, alcohol was okay in moderation – but it certainly wasn't my bezzie mate. I saw a homeopath who reminded me that we are all unique individuals, and just because my friends could handle the effects of all these toxins, it didn't mean I could.

Everybody's different. Think about it, if you give the chilled out Garfield catnip, you might find he partakes in more exercise, loses a bit of weight, and catches a few more mice. He will level out. However, give it to the already excitable Cat in the Hat and it's a whole other story.

I was basically a rather sensitive and excitable soul who was far more suited to a cup of Horlicks and a toasted teacake on a Saturday night. However, rather than putting my feet up to watch *Murder Most Horrid*, I tried to keep up with the crowd. Which meant that I was spending many Sunday mornings in floods of tears ...

'Mum, can you come and get me? I feel awful. My heart is pumping out of my chest. I need my mum. I've been stupid again.'

'I will, Lucy, but you have to stop this. You're obviously not cut out for this party lifestyle. I'll be there in half an hour.'

My mum. Always there. Always patient. Infinitely supportive and still is. Which is a good thing, considering my anxiety attacks were not confined to the 90s. Just like chokers and rubber soled platform shoes, panic made a comeback.

'...an' I said to 'er ...!'
Trying to conjure
attitude with a
Marlboro Light.

Me and my best mate
Jayne preparing for a
night out.

The years of my youth.

Faking bad. Badly.

The 90s made me do it.

I mean, look at who else was doing it back then. Look at the icons I loved who were snorting powder and smoking weed left, right and centre.

My ambitious fantasy of being the rock goddess of the village was only made stronger by watching music-inspired films like *Sid n Nancy* and *The Doors*. Live hard, die young. Talk about the tragic 27 club. Sid Vicious (Sex Pistols) and his American girlfriend Nancy Spungen were even younger than Jim Morrison and Janis Joplin when they met their makers. Oh, and who else did we lose aged 27? Nirvana's Kurt Cobain. He died 5th April 1994 of a shotgun wound to the head. His death was a suicide following years of physical illness, mental illness and addiction. And this wasn't some far away rock legend of yesteryear, this was *our* rock legend. This was *our* era. It suddenly felt real. Especially as I was hit with the news at the breakfast table by my parents, before I'd had my morning cup of tea. They had to tell a shocked teenage girl that her future husband was no more.

Yet somehow, it still felt fairly glamorous. It was still endearing. Why? Perhaps because at the time, I wanted to be a teenager with a tortured soul. Perhaps because mortality didn't register so clearly. I don't think I really believed Jim Morrison when he sang about it being "the end". After all, these stars are immortalised in history. They're legends. And whether famous or infamous, the media portrayed them as such.

In the film of their tragic lives, Sid and Nancy were played by Gary Oldman and Chloe Webb. Oldman's Sid was rather endearing – even with the vomit and the lacklustre bass playing. Webb's Nancy was a screaming, toxic banshee wrapped up tightly in PVC.

In the case of rock stars, the rebellion went a little bit further than our homemade hair dye and cigarette version. It was always drugs, wasn't it? Kurt and Courtney with their heroin. Sid and Nancy pipping them to the post with their Chelsea hotel opium pit in New York. Jim Morrison drowning in a bath reportedly with a cocktail of drugs swimming around in his blood. Drugs come with rock 'n' roll. The two go hand in hand. It's to be expected. It's just rock 'n' roll. That's what the films and newspapers told us anyway ...

Years later, after my early exposure to these tragic lives, newspaper headlines and movie portrayals, I watched more in-depth documentaries about Kurt Cobain and read all about Nancy Spungen from her mother in her book *And I Really Don't Want to Live This Life*.

Nancy. A child who suffered from night terrors and grew up with extreme mental and behavioural challenges, and a reported / debated diagnosis of schizophrenia to boot. It wasn't so much the drugs that created an imbalance in Nancy's mind, but the mental ill health that plagued her since her childhood. So perhaps she was drawn to the drugs to self-medicate, to manage whatever battles she was having within her mind? Perhaps this is why she was drawn to the anarchic punk scene? But the movie didn't tell us any of that. Sid Vicious and the Sex Pistols were the stars – Nancy was simply the loud and annoying heroin addict hanger-on, responsible for Sid's downfall. She introduced him to heroin. She was just some screeching groupie.

We didn't really need to understand Nancy's life to be entertained by that film. Who needs the person behind the caricature? That would have spoiled the angle for entertainment. It was about the Sex Pistols. It was about Sid Vicious, not his hanger-on girlfriend. I admit, it was a great film to watch, but if the truth does lie in her mother's biography, we are doing Nancy a huge disservice.

And onto my era. Did Courtney kill Kurt? Sure, why not! It's quite an exciting theory. *She* got *him* into heroin. She was loud and brash. She was his Nancy. Less famous and therefore less important. What a biatch!

But who the fuck are we to make that decision? We are unqualified judges who have never stepped foot in the same room as the people we are imposing our ill-informed verdicts on.

I've watched countless documentaries about Kurt Cobain. The one that I felt came across as most authentic was the one produced by Frances Bean Cobain – Kurt and Courtney's daughter. It's called

Montage of Heck. It showed both parents in both good and bad lights. Because with addiction – with mental illness – there can't only be good moments, can there? It felt real. Although even that film has been deemed as bullshit by some.

The point is, we have no idea who these people really are or were. We only see what the media lets us see. And there seems to be a pattern of blaming the less famous partner for limiting our catalogue of quality punk rock. So we blame somebody who we don't know and have never met before because it suits our celebrity "Big Brother" society. We watch their lives through the media and translate them as we see fit for our own entertainment. Somebody else's tragic life becomes a titbit to feed our fun and fascination.

Drugs. Conspiracy theories. Murder cases. These were the headlines associated with the stars. The words mental illness, schizophrenia, depression – they were used less often. These words sat behind the headlines. They didn't give us enough glamour or controversy. So we never associated our heroes with mental illness. We never gave their bent towards drug taking a second thought. They were rock 'n' roll. I had never even heard of the idea of self-medication through booze and drugs back then. I had no idea they might be desperately searching for some happiness or trying to numb a pain.

Meanwhile, Joe Bloggs with depression was the weirdo next door and Jane Bloggs with schizophrenia was the nutter down the road. And they *killed bunnies*!

Headlines say one thing, but real stories say something else. More recently, Amy Winehouse's ill health was played out to the public. And we lapped it up! I still feel guilty for roaring with laughter at the episode of comedy panel show *Never Mind the Buzzcocks* when she appeared blatantly drunk. It was entertaining.

But ignorance is bliss. She was doing what a lot of stars do – drinking. That's just what they do. That's all we know of them. *As if* someone famous wakes up in turmoil every day! Of course not! They've got *the life*, after all!

Who knew it was mental illness with Amy Winehouse? I didn't get it. We always wanted to see what mess she'd got herself into or how she had fucked up on stage. It's tragic. She suffered horribly and, according to the documentary *Amy*, the only reason much of that stuff played out publicly was because certain people in her life refused to let her recover in private. Her gigs, her profile – they were all too important.

When Amy Winehouse was at crisis point, the headlines included:

Amy Winehouse booed offstage

Amy Winehouse too drunk to sing

Amy Winehouse – UNBELIEVABLE (drugged and drunk)

It's enough to make you cry. And in fact, the documentary Amy did make me cry, because we got to see the real pain and distress behind the headlines. Just like so many other celebrities in pain, Amy was vilified for the only way she knew how to medicate herself. Booze and drugs.

Today, some people like mainstream TV presenter Ant McPartlin are treated with respect when they speak out about addiction. And so he should be. Were the media ever privy to any seemingly outrageous behaviour from Ant McPartlin? I have no idea. But if they were, they certainly didn't use it against him. He's one of the UK's much-loved heroes, you see. He's family TV. He isn't expected to behave in that way. Thank God he was left alone and treated with respect when the news came out though. He deserves that respect. He deserves privacy in which to recover.

But more often than not, there is certainly a lack of headlines that tackle the root cause of the problem in terms of celebrity mental ill health. Those headlines are more often reserved for unknowns who murder innocent people, or others who we only know as dangerous "mentalists". And all the people we place on pedestals? Well, in the past, we would rather have created a conspiracy theory, drama, or punk rock lifestyle around them. We didn't want to know that mental illness had anything to do with it.

Our idols were not *mentally ill*. They were living a rock 'n' roll lifestyle! Because that's what sells newspapers, right?

Wrong. It's not rock 'n' roll. And I don't like it.

In my earlier teen years, I would spend hours in my bedroom listening to Courtney Love singing 'Pretty on the Inside'. I would draw strange volcanic images with tattered angel wings sticking out from the crater, a picture of myself below. I felt muted, stifled. But now I had found artistic expression! This was *real* art. (Real art that makes me, as an adult, cringe with embarrassment, much like any song lyrics I attempted to cobble together back then. Still, art is art if it provokes a reaction, right? And I guess that can be *any* kind of reaction?)

I don't think my parents ever considered me "muted" after being continuously subjected to my screaming, which I tried to make sound croaky, Courtney-style, with a couple of cigarettes. I would then play 'Teenage Whore', spun around at 33 rpm, on my cheap plastic 90s hi-fi.

I heard my parents utter the words "strangled cat" on more than one occasion. It doesn't quite have the same ring as "tortured artist" does it? Mind you, looking back, I'm infinitely glad I was more strangled cat than tortured artist. Otherwise I might not have made it past the age of 27. The age I met the love of my life.

My lack of a shitty upbringing and my apparently sound state of mind (remember, I hadn't realised I had a mental illness back then) was really starting to bug me. I remember one day in college when I told my art lecturer, Pat (I loved Pat), that I would never amount to anything in the art world because "nothing bad has ever happened to me". She still seemed to have some kind of faith in me, though. I wasn't sure why.

Another day in class, Pat wandered over to a quiet student, whispered something to him, and then walked out of the classroom with her arm around him. We all dived around his easel like a pack of hyenas around fresh meat. What we were confronted with was not art. Our morbid fascination quickly gave way to shivers down our spines as we took in the nonsensical words falling awkwardly in a random scrawl across the page. This was never going to make a spread in The Face magazine. This had even out-edged that. And I once saw a photographic depiction of cunnilingus (what a mouthful of a word!) in that magazine. So rock 'n' roll! (We assumed everybody did that though, if they were lucky. But not everyone had hallucinations and delusions. That was some serious shit reserved for strange and curious beings, or so we thought.)

To some degree, I learnt during my A Levels that not all artists are eccentric and wild. Some seemed merely attention seeking, constantly talking about how deep and tortured their personal worlds were.

I remember feeling furious when students and teachers alike pandered to one of the girls in class. She stood up to discuss her painting and cried because of something or other – it wasn't clear and it's certainly not burnt in my memory. Sure, she might have had a tough time, but it felt so contrived, so attention seeking to me at the time. Meanwhile, there was a guy living with AIDS who quietly created masterpieces but didn't score as highly with the lecturers because he didn't share his *process*. He had shit going on, but kept it to himself other than conveying it through real, fine art.

On reflection I know that I was being incredibly judgmental about the crying girl. I never asked her anything directly. I just *assumed* she was contrived, which is wrong. This may well have been the only way she felt comfortable discussing whatever it was that was bothering her. It may have been an authentic way of reaching out to someone – her way. Maybe she just needed to talk. Good on her, actually.

Other students were pop-punk party animals who teamed a baggy pair of jeans with a well-worn pair of Vans. I liked them. They seemed to head towards the worlds of graphic design and photography. And they were SO. MUCH. FUN. Going clubbing with this lot was a positive way to spend my time.

Others were more bubble gum pop, with perms à la Kylie Minogue circa 1987, and a permanent smile painted across their faces. They seemed a little out of place at art college, but I liked them too. I would never have imagined any of them having a mental illness. Stigma. Again.

Some students were authentically quirky. Some, like the guy with the easel and the sprawling words, lived with mental ill health.

Oh my god – he was actually a mentally ill person! Right there, in our class, in the same room as us. All of a sudden, I felt slightly on edge. Because what did I know of mentally ill people? They murdered bunnies and stuck stilettos in your boyfriend's eye. They wanted to marry their feline friends which was like *totally fucked up*!

After walking out that day, he never came back in. Which makes me think that whatever happened during that class wasn't an artistic profusion to paper, but a psychotic symptom of an unknown illness. Unknown to us, that is. It was the college gossip of the day, beating (by a mile) that girl who wore the 80s style leather jacket and told us tales of coming to college straight from A&E following a heroin overdose.

But then mental illness happened to a good friend of mine. She was an artist. So when she started hugging strangers, nobody thought much of it. She was eccentric. She was so much fun and really interesting and quirky, all I had ever wanted to be. But then things got out of hand.

She was sectioned.

She wasn't the only person we knew with mental ill health. There were other friends, all of whom had hallucinations and delusions in common. It wasn't like something out of a Doors movie. It wasn't like something from the *Magic Roundabout*. And it didn't automatically allow you to sell out an arena gig or produce a priceless masterpiece. It wasn't nice. It wasn't fun. People suffered. People were sectioned. It was sad.

Soon I came to the had this realisation that art, drugs, and eccentricity aren't always what they seem. And living on the edge certainly isn't as glamorous as my naïve mind had once thought.

The day I walked out of art college, never to return, was review day. It wasn't with Pat (I will always love Pat!) but two male lecturers – the same two who empathised with crying girl (let me apologise again if there was more than spilt milk going on there – my teenage arrogance may well have been oblivious to it). Anyway, I presented my work.

In graphic art, we had to choose a shape – a circle, square or triangle – and create a series of cards from it. I chose a circle, and based my project on alcohol.

There were images of the inviting bubbles in the beer, peering into the bottom of the empty glass, taking a bite from a forbidden apple, having the spikiest mother of all headaches, and then finally finishing with an image of a washing machine depicting regret, the morning after and, quite literally, the often-immediate desire to wash everything you'd been out in. I wrapped it in a homemade packet of bubble wrap because, after all, alcohol stops you from seeing clearly. It was supposed to be pretty light-hearted. Humorous, even. Fun. Perhaps that's why it didn't go down too well.

'Are you having problems at home?'

That's what I was asked at my review. With my lecturers blatantly unimpressed with my teenage artwork, and asking uninvited questions about my family life (which was still absolutely fine, by the way), I picked up my portfolio and dragged my hungover carcass out of that review meeting and into the pub. I never went back.

Why shouldn't I have made light of what sometimes made me feel terrible? Why shouldn't I have tried to look at it through a different, more amusing lens?

After walking out of college, I ended up working in a pub, a little extension of my gap between college and career. It wasn't a great place for a socially awkward girl – you certainly couldn't drink when on duty, so I often became the butt of the jokes.

'Lucy, will you pop outside into the beer garden and grab me some fresh herbs? They're growing just by the bins.'

'Sure.'

Naïvety and awkwardness were not great attributes for working in a bar or pub kitchen. But then, making light of life was apparently not a great character trait for fine art either.

No, there were no problems in the family home (not that I knew about anyway). And my mental illness wasn't alcohol related. I just liked a drink when I went out. Sure, I couldn't handle it and felt full of regret the next morning, but that was standard stuff really.

Problems at home? What a presumption!

Back to the point. The media was telling me that the successful, talented, creative individuals who were heading into a downfall were simply eccentric and rock 'n' roll. And the mentally ill people were those dangerous characters in horror movies and the weird guys down the road. But as I discovered, this was simply stereotyping.

The mentally ill people were the people in college, the friends who I hung out at the pub with. They were me …

I had a mental health disorder. I can see that now.

CHAPTER 5

Stereotype: The Toxic Triffid

REALITY: THE WILTING WALLFLOWER

By the mid-noughties I was in my mid-twenties and not the wallflower I used to be. On the outside, anyway. My inner wallflower lived on, but I tried my damnedest to portray a triffid instead. Confused? Let me explain. Triffids are highly toxic, fictional plants that kill people. I myself was highly toxic when I portrayed a triffid. And I shot looks that could kill. It took copious amounts of alcohol to get my triffid game face on.

So this is what often happens when you're socially anxious: you come across as aloof, aggressive or arrogant, when deep down you're freaking out about how you look, how you hold your cigarette, how clumsy you appear when some nice guy comes over to talk to you, whether you have bad breath or if you have something green stuck in your teeth. So the best defence? Slap on your best bitch face and say very little, because you "just don't care."

The other thing is, you appear to have a bigger ego than Donald Trump. You appear to be constantly seeking compliments. Remember the narcissist? Yes, it's true, I am constantly looking for compliments. But not so that I can chuck them on top of my great big tower of ego. It's so I can chuck them in the bottomless empty void that is my confidence. Of course, as I've mentioned before, once you chuck in a compliment in the form of external validation, it falls through the hole because there's absolutely nothing for it to latch on to. So you seek out more. And every time you find validation, it runs away again and you stop believing you ever really had it. And on it goes.

I think this may be a factor in some of the issues I have had with people: a lack of confidence that probably appears as incompetence, coupled with constant demands for an ego boost which make me look like an arrogant twat with no substance.

So do the maths. Throw in the external validation requirement, the seeming lack of competence and attach the toxic triffid bitch face and you probably have a fairly unlikeable character.

Switching from wallflower to triffid never really did me any favours in terms of my Friday night quest to "pull" a nice, suitable boyfriend.

I got far more attention from the boys when I gave off the sweet smell of shyness and, well, just being quite nice.

People who knew me well knew that I was really just socially awkward. But if they didn't, my aura was arrogance with a hint of narcissism.

I'm lucky this fake drunken arrogance didn't get me into too much bother over the years. It certainly got me close a few times though …

'She just fucking looked at me funny!' said the equally pissed girl outside Pozition nightclub – only with a bit more conviction in her menacing eyes than I had obviously managed to conjure up in my own. Because it became apparent that I didn't faze her. Not one bit. I might have stood my ground, I might have got a push and shove in there, I might have taken part in the ensuing handbag-and-heels streetside battle, but I'm not sure I would have walked away quite so unscathed if my 5ft 11 friend wasn't with me. Inside, I wasn't quite so confident. My friend, however, was a secondary school teacher in one of Hull's toughest areas. This was nowt to her.

And it's interesting that when the police turned up to the scene of the pathetic scuffle, they held the girl with menacing eyes and her mate back and then waved us on. I don't think we really gave off the aroma of trouble. Just a whiff of menthol ciggies, Blue WKD and being in the wrong place at the wrong time.

Weeks later, sitting in the Hull Truck Theatre press office, I picked up the phone.

'Hi Lucy, it's Ricky from Pozition.'

As Bridget Jones might say:
Fuuuuuuuuuuuuuuuuuuuuuuuuuuuuuuuuuuuuuuuuuuck!

Ricky was the owner of the nightclub. And the weekend before, I'd argued with his bouncers for about 15 minutes, demanding to be let in after 1am. For about five of those minutes, they said no, and then one of them recognised one of the actors we were with. Having an actor in your party was like having the secret password.

Open sesame.

But I was still seething at the earlier "you're not coming in" line. *Nobody* said no to me! It was deeply cutting to a self-loather. (Who?! Exactly! Who the fuck am I anyway?!)

So I decided to stay behind for another ten minutes, letting the bemused doormen / women know that this slightly slurry 20-something wasn't at all happy at the initial rejection. It was a monotonous whine on a loop.

Back to Ricky.

'You obviously bring good guests to the club. But I can't have you arguing the toss with my staff in the streets every week. In future, here's my number. Call me first and I will make sure you can come straight in without a fuss.'

It sounds kind of cool. But it wasn't. He wasn't happy. And it wasn't because I was special. It was because I often had a soap star in tow from the theatre, which was kind of my job. They weren't in my personal social set.

I thanked him. 'Cheers, Ricky. I'll make sure I do that.'

It wasn't the first time I had had a run in with a bouncer. It became a Friday night pastime. And often, embarrassingly, a spectator sport.

When I tried to be "nice" and assertive, it didn't work either. I had no idea how to flirt. It would usually involve staring at somebody I fancied, with a look that said "I want to kill you." Or it would involve swaying to the Cretan bar in Malia with double vision, and asking the barman (or woman – I couldn't really see straight) for a snog.

'No. You need to leave. And can you take your friend with you – she's puked spaghetti bolognaise all over the floor and people are having to step over it.'

Before my husband, Chris, got to know me, he thought I hated him. I had a crush on this man for years before we eventually hit it off, but as you might imagine, the insecurity manifested itself in total arsehole, up-yourself triffid behaviour.

One thing I loved doing as a single girl working in a theatre was grabbing the casting files full of actors' headshots, to see who was incoming for the shows. Everything was done in hard copy in those days – photographs were not emailed from agents; they were posted. And I, in turn, as the marketing and press officer, posted them onto the printers to produce the programmes. (Yes – and I am, sadly, old enough to have been given a typewriter in my first office job. Sorry? You don't know what a typewriter is? Oh, right, it's a mechanical box with keys, a ribbon and a slot to put paper in. Seems like worlds away now, doesn't it?)

So I would flick through the manila files and the enclosed 10 x 8s to see who was going to be my Heathcliff, my Prince Charming, my Stuart the baker …

It was Stuart the baker who I fell for. But when I first saw my dream actor's photo, I thought, *no way*! He looked far too young. However, I was later to discover that this was because this guy was so disorganised, he had used a headshot from his early 20s because he hadn't got round to renewing them. He was actually 30. He was also a Geordie (swoon – who doesn't love a North East Geordie accent?) And when he arrived at our *Cooking with Elvis* meet and greet (where he was to play Stuart the baker in Lee Hall's bloody brilliant dark comedy) I was seriously wowed. I can still remember seeing him in the theatre foyer, wandering over to the welcome cakes with his cuppa, before settling down with a roll-up cigarette (which were allowed in the workplace in those days) and listening to us all take it in turns to say who we were and what we did for the theatre.

'Hi. I'm Chris. I play Stuart.'

'Hi. I'm Lucy. I'm the Press Officer.'

Cringe.

So what should a girl, who falls instantly for one of the cast, do?

That's right. Ignore him.

Turns out he thought I was a bit of an arrogant cow who, for whatever reason, took a strong dislike to him. He just couldn't understand what he had done to me or how he had offended me.

I saw him in the green room one day when I went to make a cuppa. I walked in, glanced at the TV screen, acknowledged that *Neighbours* was on by saying 'Uh, *Neighbours*,' (possibly with a forced upward inflection as we all did after consuming a diet of after-school Aussie soaps) and then proceeded to make a cuppa with my back to him the entire time.

My mouth said 'Uh, Neighbours.'

My body language said 'I don't like you one little bit.'

My mind said 'Oh my god. I'm in the green room with Chris Connel. Could this be it? Might he ask me out? What can I say? Oh my god, I am going to totally embarrass myself. But I really want to go on a date with him, marry him, and have his babies.'

I'd already dreamt about autumn nights on a Tyneside beach, drinking cans and smoking roll-ups. Marriage and babies was obviously the next natural step.

Instead, I walked out with a half-smile, kicking myself at another wasted opportunity.

So the next time I saw him in the green room I tried a bit harder. But I ended up telling him a seriously uninteresting story about finding a butternut squash in the back of my wardrobe.

So now he thinks I'm arrogant with a wardrobe full of rotting, middle class fruit. Great.

I went back to my original approach. I bumped into him in the local supermarket. His digs were not too far from my home, so there was always the opportunity / risk (depending on the mood I was in) of bumping into him. I said hi, instantly panicked, and ran down the nearest aisle, forgetting my shopping basket. This forced me to retrace my steps carefully without being seen and dive back down said aisle with my heart pounding and my face burning.

So nothing happened that year. Or the year after. Or the year after that. I remained single for the foreseeable, thanks to my resting bitch face and seemingly uninterested conversation. And possibly the rotting fruit story.

Being single and having anxiety meant that I had to put this stupid act on every time I went out. I continued to repel men. Well, the decent ones anyway. But that was okay. I hadn't embarrassed myself, because from the look on my face I wasn't interested anyway.

Every Friday night I went back to Hull's least hip club, where I argued with the bouncers and fearfully fought with the girls. It was R&B night. (What the fuck happened to me? I used to have half-decent taste in music – not that my mother would agree. 'This is just noise, Lucy!')

Armed with a Smirnoff Ice and a Marlboro Menthol, I would make my way to the second-floor dance floor and shake my booty like Beyoncé. This is where the extroverted narcissism of the intoxicated kind comes into play, I guess. What a fool! I thought I was a seriously good dancer. I felt irresistible. I was seriously going for it in my high heels and oversized hoop earrings from Claire's Accessories. I was fuelled – and fooled – by vodka.

I can only imagine I looked a right tit.

I got attention. But I doubt that was because I did a fine impression of Beyoncé. I think it was probably more to do with how drunk I looked and how short my skirt was. Attention of the wrong kind.

The problem is, you lose your self-respect when the only guys you attract are the overconfident ones with one thing on their minds. Not good – especially when all I really wanted was a nice boyfriend to watch *Friends* re-runs with while eating pizza on a Friday night.

However, the appeal of creating my own fictional kick-ass persona – mixed with a pinch of tortured soul and a smidgen of rebellion – was really rather endearing. When you grow up admiring Courtney Love rather than Posh Spice, your attitude is far more important than your designer label.

CHAPTER 6

Appearance: The Globetrotter

REALITY: THE GIRL ON THE RUN

Okay, so "the globetrotter" isn't exactly a mental health stereotype. But, at the end of the day, it *is* relevant. Because while I fooled myself and everyone else about my confidence and independence with extravagant and impulsive travel plans, I wasn't much of a fan of myself and of my life generally. I was running away from it. And my anxiety was fuelled that. In fact, I was fuelled by about as much anxiety as the Boeing 747 was fuelled by kerosene. I was carrying a hell of a lot of it – even though I pretended to myself, and to others, that I wasn't.

It wasn't just caffeine that would create feelings of terror whenever I travelled abroad, which makes me wonder why on Earth I ran to the other side of the world to try to make myself feel better.

Back in my teens and early twenties, whenever I planned to go to Crete, or Spain, or Morocco, or anywhere else that felt significantly warmer than Blighty, I had a pre-trip panic about the heat. Could I breathe in the heat? Would it suffocate me and burn my lungs? I would do everything I could to seek out air conditioning before booking a trip, but it wasn't usually affordable within my budget back then. So I'd happily spend far too many euros hiring an over-priced fan for the bedroom that simply pushed the hot air around the room, but somehow made me feel better with the breeze. There was a fine line between a breeze and a choking wind though.

Morocco. I was on the strictest of missions to avoid contracting stomach bugs through ingestion (no ice cubes, no washed salad), which was pretty much impossible. Imagine my horror of getting back on a bus of doom while already feeling on edge – but this time with the prospect of a nine-hour journey, blazing heat, no on-board toilet, and just one Imodium to keep my pretty maxi dress clean for the entire journey. It was hell – but I survived it. And so did my maxi dress.

We (and by we, I mean me and Candy Flip guy) travelled through Ketama where young children ran to the bus, banging their fists on the windows shouting 'Hashish, hashish!' We didn't buy. Although perhaps, on reflection, it might have chilled me out a bit.

We were due to get off at a little mountain village called Chefchaouen, but the seasoned Belgian travellers we met on the bus warned us that it was not a good place to stay. My travel guide said differently and boasted of its beautiful blue-rinsed buildings. But with a stomach still gurgling and the sounds of children selling "hashish" still ringing in my ears, I wasn't up for taking any chances. Shame. It did look beautiful.

We carried on towards a town called Tétouan instead – which was seriously stressful, as it turned out. We were followed around by people who demanded money from us because we had unwittingly tried on Moroccan clothes and asked for directions, not realising that it cost us money to do so.

After that awful experience we found solace in a lovely little town called Martil. It was beautiful and we met a wonderful Moroccan lad called Ahmed who befriended us, showed us around and told us all about Moroccan culture. It was a truly lush few days and I started to relax, enjoy myself and take in what was all around me. The heat was something else though!

When we reached the tourist resort of Tanjer on the last leg of the trip and the heat died down, I breathed a sigh of relief. The breeze. What lovely breeze. You'd think that would ease any remnants of anxiety. But the breeze was getting stronger. It wasn't so nice anymore. As though I was in a skydive with ongoing freefall, I felt like I couldn't breathe and the air was being forced up my nose and into my mouth at high speed. And not only couldn't I breathe, this weather system felt like something out of that Twister movie. Except I wasn't as brave as actress Helen Hunt. The sooner I could hide from the breeze of doom with a gin and tonic, the better. The plush bar we rounded our budget trip off with certainly helped. But all in all, it seemed that change and new experiences and cultures – anything that gave me an air of uncertainty – were more nerve-wracking than exciting.

Years later, aged 24, feeling miserable and searching for … something, I decided to leave the country. I was going to be independent, strong and confident. A self-assured globetrotter who was doing it for herself. I was going to be strong and embrace change, cultures and uncertainty.

Well. Not exactly.

Amazingly, I made it to New Zealand without having any illegal drugs stashed in my belongings whatsoever (everybody was a suspected drugs trafficker in my eyes – I'd seen the film *Bangkok Hilton* with Nicole Kidman and I knew I couldn't endure prison). My flight socks appeared to work, as I didn't collapse with DVT (pacing the flight every hour and necking aspirin also mitigated that risk) and my fabulous Irish friend met me at the airport as arranged.

I had a place to stay, a new job to start and a theatre show to see that evening (it was Caligula. If you've not yet seen it don't worry – I think there will be a modern-day version of the same story called Trump coming soon).

I was full of excitement. I was slightly disappointed that I didn't fancy any of my new housemates, but they probably thought the same about me. The only thing that got me down was missing my lovely little cats when I woke up in the morning without their furry, purry cuddles.

But it was great. At first.

I lasted about eight weeks working for the theatre company in Auckland. I had become shy again, unable to converse. I stayed fairly mute in the office – and thanked God for the generous offerings of pavlova that my talented colleagues brought in. At least there were reasons not to have to speak when you're stuffing your face with this fabulous New Zealand dessert (or was it Australian? There was an ongoing row over that one down under).

I was restless. I wasn't living the lifestyle I had imagined – it was the same as home but with a different backdrop, flip flops and fewer friends.

Perhaps it was where we were living? Colleagues at the theatre told me there wasn't much going on where I was staying. They said I should really be looking to stay in Ponsonby or Parnell.

My Irish friend took me out to Mission Bay one Saturday and I loved it. I was desperate to live somewhere like Mission Bay – a seaside town with nice restaurants and loads of people buzzing around. Still, I didn't feel happy while I was there on my day trip, so the fact that I believed I would be happy if I moved there full-time was perhaps a little ambitious.

Maybe I needed to move around more quickly? Keep the anxiety demons at bay?

I handed in my notice and hopped on a Stray Travel adventure bus to journey around the North Island. It was great fun, always moving and meeting new travellers as we dropped off and picked up at different stops along the route. I was convinced I was going to fall in love with some perfect, cosmic traveller.

I didn't.

And while writing this, I am incredibly disappointed in myself that my entire trip was based on this notion. Caitlin Moran I was not! Feminism obviously wasn't something I had grasped at that time.

It was an interesting trip. Looking back, I'm glad I did it and it's hard to get my head around the fact that I was never content. I stepped barefoot onto the soft warm sand of the beautifully picturesque Cathedral Cove; I enjoyed drinking cold beer and paddling in the hot pools we made on Hot Water Beach; I ventured onto the active ground of the Thermal Village in Rotorua where we got up close to an active geyser and watched mud bubbling of its own accord. It was awesome. But it wasn't enough.

I was not happy. At all. I got drunk whenever I could, woke up feeling rubbish and had to find something else to keep my mind active. Nothing worked. I felt lonely.

Me and Kat sightseeing in Australia behind thick beer goggles.

So I made my excuses and left the trip early. I headed back to Auckland. I felt more bored, lonelier, and more miserable than before, so within a week, I hopped on another Stray bus and headed north to Paihia and the Bay of Islands. Luckily on this trip I met the fabulous Kat, who was to become a close friend and travelling ally. She wasn't a magic pill for happiness and contentment – my anxiety didn't totally disappear, but she took my mind off it somewhat.

We instantly clicked. We partied together, shopped together and visited historic sites together. She had travelled from Vancouver where she had just gone through a divorce (albeit an amicable one) and was rapidly draining the money she made on her house like it was burning a hole in the pockets of her Roxy shorts.

We had come from different backgrounds and countries, but the same sort of things made us giggle. Still, I couldn't relax into the travel diary journaling or Dan Brown pages like she could. Kat had just gone through a divorce, but she seemed far more content and far more comfortable in her own company. I still couldn't relax.

At the end of the trip I headed back to Auckland, had a big blowout with Kat and a slightly more conservative girl we met (lush, but sensible), and then I headed back to my room in the shared house for the festive season.

My ex-soldier ex-boyfriend flew out from Australia to see me for Christmas. I was excited to see him, but I didn't have high hopes. I remember my mum texting me, asking if I was looking forward to it. I responded saying "yeah", but that it was "going to be a complete disaster." I sent it to him by accident (it must have been the previous night's endless pints of Speights lager still flooding my brain with alcohol). Anyway, he came, and I spent the entire time feeling on edge. I made everyone's life hell by getting too drunk and being a total arse on a night out over Christmas. When was I going to learn that I couldn't handle my beer?

He flew back to Sydney on New Year's Eve and I was annoyed with myself that he hadn't fallen hopelessly in love with my charms (introverted narcissism again – I was absolutely not charming).

I was also working out a lot and watching what I ate. I actually bought a new TV and searched high and low for a DVD player that would let me play my UK Nell McAndrew Maximum Impact workout disc. I was thin. I know I was thin. But at the time I felt like I needed to do something to make me better and happier. If one thing didn't work, I looked for something else to fill the void.

But calorie counting and excessive workouts never made anyone happy.

If only life could be transformed by an actual head switch. Happiness on, misery off. Hypnotherapy had to be the nearest thing to a switch, so I did my research.

I told my housemates all about it after my first session. I had found some random hypnotherapist in the directory and caught the bus over to her home in a strange suburb I had never ventured into before. I carried her address – which was scribbled in biro on a small scrap of paper – in my nervous, sweaty palm.

I arrived at the house, entered and sat down cautiously in her wicker chair.

I couldn't help thinking that some crazed killer might emerge from the kitchen brandishing a bread knife while I was "under". Nobody knew where I was. And remember, I'd seen all the horror movies by this point. I had some pretty good ideas of what could happen to me.

What if, like Julia Roberts, my hypnotherapist was also "sleeping with the enemy"? What if her mentally ill husband was lurking in the pantry among the neatly lined tins of baked beans and tuna fish, ready to pounce while I was vulnerable? What if I never left this house again? What if they made a film about me?

Naïve British traveller, in search of happiness, meets grisly end while semi-conscious in a stranger's wicker chair.

Oh God. But it would be far too embarrassing to up and leave now …

So, I did my best to relax. After all, I had a "smoking habit" to kick. (It was a habit, certainly, but I wasn't addicted. I just had very little self-control when I was drunk. And because I wasn't especially happy, I was very drunk quite a lot of the time.)

I had told the hypnotist that I was there to "quit smoking", when really I was there for my anxiety and unhappiness. When I got there, I just shoehorned the seemingly random add-on that I wanted to exhibit more confidence – perhaps she could do some work on that too?

I managed not to smoke that night, even after drinking a few too many pints of Speights and tequila shots. I think my confidence went up a notch too – but I'm not sure the hypnotherapist could take credit for that.

Of course, once the Mexican toxins had vacated my body, my mind was left feeling shitty once more. So I found another hypnotherapist (I'm not sure why I needed a different one, especially given that I had survived the first session. There was seemingly no tin-straightening crazy husband and my body hadn't been left cut to shreds in a wicker chair).

The next one was in another strange suburb. I have no idea what I got from that, other than a bit of arm tapping, affirmation chanting and – weirdly, for no apparent reason – a deluge of tears.

Things only got worse when I left for the South Island. I won't go into detail, but it's safe to say I had a fair bit of fun while I was travelling – as any single girl might. But in behaving the way I was accustomed to, my self-respect was at an all-time low.

My face was covered in spots, I was rundown, and my mum kept asking me to return home. I didn't. But the entire time I was in Christchurch I spent at least three hours every day sitting in the internet cafe in town, googling "jaw surgery".

When I was younger I was told I had an overbite. I didn't realise I had one. I hadn't noticed anything wrong with my face until the dentist told me. However, I didn't get it fixed as I was more ashamed of wearing the head brace than I was of the overbite. Years later, however, that imperfection came back to haunt me. I became completely and utterly obsessed with my jaw line during my trip.

I asked any professional I met about the procedure. I lived with two Irish doctors. They thought I was being silly. I remember one of them saying 'Can't you just hold it in place if that's what's bothering you?' I met a physiotherapist and asked her about it too. Her view was 'If it's not broken, don't try to fix it.' They all infuriated me. How could they not see what a huge problem this was? I had the side profile of Marge bloody Simpson.

My view remained unchanged. My ugly face with its spots, its hungover red eyes, and its vile and ugly jaw line seemed to be the root cause of my unhappiness. After all, Stray Bus trips, being thin and beautiful coastlines hadn't changed anything.

So, sitting in the internet cafe, with the sun shining through the window – reminding me that I should actually be thrilled to be alive and excitedly exploring the land of *Lord of the Rings*, rather than obsessing about how ugly I was – I checked out other people's stories of jaw surgery online. Google strikes again. I searched for places that could perform it; I looked up costs and payment options. I weighed up whether or not the post-op challenges – like being unable to eat anything other than soup for weeks or thinking you were going to choke when being sick because you couldn't open your wired-up jaw far enough – were, in fact worth it. I considered having the work done in another country; I considered whether wearing the train track braces for two or three years would be worth it.

I was unsure, so I decided to do something else in my pursuit of happiness. While sitting in that internet cafe, I booked more travel. Instead of going home when I was meant to (i.e. after three months) I booked flights to Fiji, Australia, and New York. I was convinced it was my destiny to become a Carrie Bradshaw type, living it up with fabulous new best friends in Manhattan. Cosmopolitans, shopping trips to Bloomingdales and making a name for myself in the Big Apple. Ha. It's hilarious, looking back. I really don't fancy that. Carrie Bradshaw is a knob.

Before I left though, there was one last thing I needed to do. I needed to jump out of a plane. It was kind of like some sort of traveller's rite of passage. Everyone had done it. If I didn't, I'd be a failure. A travelling let-down. An amateur.

I booked it and spent the night before wide awake, wondering if I would ever make it home again. I made the early morning call to check it was going ahead (a weather check) and it was still on. I was leaping out of that plane whether I liked it or not. And I bloody did it.

The freefall wasn't frightening because I was in the air. The ground was so far away it didn't feel real. And the blast of air shooting up around me took away any feeling of "falling". But the air that rushed through my nostrils made me feel as though I couldn't breathe – just like in Morocco. Still, I remained conscious throughout and hit the ground with only a slight bump.

Sadly, however, it wasn't life-changing. But I guess it was a quick-fix buzz all the same. I felt nerves, I felt excitement, I felt exhilaration. I drank champagne with the two girls from London who leapt from the same plane. But it didn't last for long.

Soon I was on the move again – running away from another place of unhappiness.

First stop – paradise; the beautiful island of Fiji for a well-earned chill out in the most gorgeous of surroundings. Well, it was certainly stunning. I met an amazing group of people. But I was B.O.R.E.D, wishing the days away, desperate for something to happen. It didn't. That was supposed to be the point though. For most people, anyway.

There was always a hammock rush first thing – you know, like staking your claim on the sun beds with your beach towels. A hammock was the best place to relax and read a book, occasionally looking up from under your straw hat to see the sun's rays sparkling on the still blue water. Once you got that hammock, you didn't give it up. Except for me – I lasted about an hour before searching for something else to do. It's not that I don't like relaxing and reading. These days, it's pretty much all I do. But perhaps that's because I'm happier and more content with life (to a point). I no longer need to be constantly running away from anything or running towards something new.

Next stop was Melbourne. Why did I choose Melbourne? Because soldier boy said he didn't like it. And I couldn't risk going to Sydney for fear of bumping into him (you know how big Sydney is, right? I guess I was slightly paranoid ...).

Melbourne was the home of *Neighbours*. It was going to be my saviour, my ticket to a healthy, and happy beach lifestyle. Barbecues with my new neighbours in the back garden. Bliss.

Except it wasn't.

My itchy feet had me living in three different places in just one week. First thing I did when I got to Melbourne was pick up a copy of *The Age* and look at the classifieds for a place to stay. I spent the first two nights in The Base hostel in St Kilda. While there, I looked at a place to stay up the road in Balaclava – the other side of the bustling and seriously cool Carlisle Street. They had a few people to see and 'interview' but I couldn't wait. So I found another place – in the suburbs.

In a cab with the Aussie Hero petrol station burger.
You make bad choices when you've had a drink.

Oh my god, this could be like a real-life Erinsborough![5] My own version of Ramsey Street.

I was so convinced this was the right thing to do that I said I would take the room, jumped in a taxi and moved in. But it wasn't Ramsey Street. Jason and Kylie didn't live there. And so when I heard from the girl from Balaclava 36 hours later, I made my excuses and jumped on a train back to the city.

I met and made some amazing friends. I was back in touch with Kat, the Canadian friend I made on the Stray Bus in NZ. She also moved into the gorgeous house in Balaclava. Our household included a great couple from Perth and a girl from Newcastle in the UK. I got a job in recruitment and had ticked every box.

Friends. Tick.

Home. Tick.

Job. Tick. I have never been diagnosed with depression (although it was recently hinted at by a therapist. They didn't want to label me, but they brought up the possibility and my need for self-care). But looking back on this trip, I do wonder if I was somewhat depressed. Or perhaps I was just homesick. It's hard to know, but the jaw obsession and the unhappiness and the constant restlessness were definitely not right. I dreaded spending even one night in on my own. I couldn't bear to be alone. I forced everyone to watch British movies and they struggled to understand the accents in every single Guy Ritchie film ever made. I longed for home but at the same time hated the idea of returning to it having failed in my pursuit of happiness. Every night out was filled with hope and anticipation that always, always failed to live up to expectations. I signed up to about four different dance classes – belly dancing, street dancing, salsa dancing, and pole dancing – but I didn't stick any of them out. I shopped like crazy in Melbourne's fashionable Prahran, I dined in the finest restaurants and, unlike other travellers, I lived in a beautiful home with two balconies, for Christ's sake!

5 The suburb in which the Australian soap opera Neighbours is set. It's not a real place!

I was in Melbourne, a fantastic and welcoming city. And, yet again, I was miserable.

My gums were bleeding, so I convinced myself I had HIV. I spent hundreds of dollars visiting GPs, having STD tests that came back negative (I read that bleeding gums could be a sign of HIV). But I didn't do the specific HIV test while I was away – that was far too scary for my anxious mind to contend with, given that, with my bleeding gums, it was highly likely I had contracted it at some point in my life. I therefore saved that one for later. But don't worry, that came back negative too, as my GP advised was the likely outcome. I still nearly passed out with anxiety at the hospital, prompting the nurse to advise me to lie down while she fetched me a sugary drink because I had gone as white as a ghost.

Oh, and I forgot to mention, this all came on the back of having already spent hundreds of NZ dollars on all that hypnotherapy in Auckland, where I was desperate to find some form of spiritual happiness through reflection or something. What a load of bollocks.

Eventually I gave up on all that and dabbled with MDMA again. Perhaps the Aussie version was going to be cleaner and more like a giant cuddle than the grotty UK version? Wrong again. It was just as grotty, just as sleazy.

Nothing made me happy.

I could spend the day walking among the most beautiful scenery and feel numb. No, not numb – it was restlessness that dominated me. I was so restless I couldn't take in what was around me. I remember visiting the Royal Botanical Gardens in the centre of Melbourne with Kat, and yet I wasn't able to enjoy a single second. It was 38 hectares containing over 50,000 plants, representing 8,500 different species. God, how much would I love to wander among all of that today! The only thing I can remember about it is my friend taking tons of carefully considered photos while I just stood and watched. Oh, and I also remember the walk back towards the tram, feeling disappointed that I hadn't enjoyed all the good stuff that Australia had to offer. Again.

It was the same with coastal views from the Great Ocean Road. That didn't work either.

Or seeing the animals at Melbourne Zoo.

Or wandering around St Kilda's Luna Park.

None of it worked.

A trip along the Great Ocean Road, Victoria.

I'm smiling on all of the photos, but inside I was so unsettled and miserable during that time. Nothing could fix it. I'm not claiming that I was thoroughly depressed, by a long stretch. I just had this horrible nagging feeling inside and I was always antsy – always looking for something else. I didn't feel especially connected to people, I didn't feel especially connected to my surroundings and I didn't feel connected to conversations. It was as though my brain was always looking for something more. It couldn't live in the now, not ever. Basically, I endured the daytimes in anticipation of the night times – looking forward to drinking, dancing and being someone else for a few hours. I wanted to be the 'someone' I was supposed to be – the confident young traveller who was having the time of her life.

It wasn't just Melbourne either. I packed up and headed off to Sydney, and then to Perth – thinking another move would help. It didn't. I simply could not outrun the sadness or the anxiety.

I sat in the sunshine, drinking iced coffee against the backdrop of the Sydney Opera House (yes, I did make it there eventually, albeit very briefly and constantly looking over my shoulder). I came face-to-face with an unbelievably cute little Thorny Devil on the dusty roads of Western Australia. I hand-fed Lucy, the 18-month-old kangaroo. Well, the baby kangaroo encounter worked, but only briefly.

I thought maybe New York would be different. After all, it felt like it would be more like home, without having to be exactly the same as home. I knew home didn't hold the key to happiness. The Australian climate didn't warrant as many roast dinners and the sun was a little on the strong side for my alabaster and spotty skin. In New York I was bound to find mashed potato and a bit of comforting drizzle. New York offered me a brand new window of hope.

I should make clear at this point that every single person I met on my travels (apart from a couple of nasty blokes in the pub who spat venom – but you get that everywhere) did everything they possibly could to make me feel welcome. I would love to go back to all of the places I visited and see them with new eyes.

My mum thought I was the luckiest girl on Earth meeting all these fabulous people. I met Clare and Ben in Melbourne, who put me in touch with Lana in Perth. I met Stacey in Christchurch who put me in touch with Megan and Doug and Danny in NYC. Everywhere I went there was a friendly face to greet me. It couldn't have gone more smoothly in that respect.

So having landed in NYC, Megan gave me instructions of how to find her apartment and exactly what to say to the taxi driver so he didn't instantly know I was a tourist and charge me double. I arrived at Megan's apartment block where she greeted me with a big American smile and a vodka cranberry. This girl was amazing. I had really landed on my feet here. We knocked back the vodka cranberries and headed to the Port Authority station where we were met by her lovely friend Danny. Then we hopped on a bus and headed to Atlantic City to stay with Megan's family for her little sister's 21st. The whole group made me feel so welcome, bought me salt water taffy and entertained me with blackjack and wine.

New Yorkers are the business.

When we returned to Manhattan, Megan and Danny had to work (both are lawyers) so Megan's mum visited from Pennsylvania and took me out for lunch and on a shopping trip around Manhattan. I spent most of my time in Manhattan staying with Megan's other friend, Doug, who was out of town on business for most of the time, but was more than happy to have a cat lover looking after his two lovely kitties.

I was living it up like Carrie Bradshaw in a lush apartment all to myself on the Upper West Side. The only problem was, I had indigestion for the first few days, so I had to do quite a bit of online searching to ensure I wasn't dying of stomach or oesophageal cancer. About half way through my two-week trip, I decided that I wasn't dying and relaxed a little bit, just enough to do a movie location tour. I loved seeing the *Ghostbusters* offices in Tribeca (I can just hear Janine's voice now – 'Ghostbusters, what d'ya want?')

As my trip home fast approached I started to look forward to it. After all, the actor I was crazy in love with was about to resume his role as Stuart the baker at our theatre, so really, it didn't matter that I was returning to the UK a single woman. Chris Connel was going to grace the stage with a fake tortoise and a tight Elvis suit once again. Hooray!

Hope springs eternal.

CHAPTER 7

Stereotype: The Neurotic Stepmother

REALITY: THE CHILDLIKE PARENT

Chris (aka Stuart the baker) was a single parent. I suppose, *officially*, he was a single step-parent as he isn't Sam's biological father (as if I needed another reason to fall madly in love with him, he took on somebody else's child and loved him unconditionally as his own. Swoon). But he had been Sam's dad since he was a baby, and that means more than matching blood groups in my eyes.

Finally, after years of my daydreaming and lusting after him, we got together at the Hull Truck Theatre Christmas party in 2005. Apparently, he hadn't been turned off by my severely lacking conversational skills about rotting fruit in wardrobes. He had, by all accounts, been thinking about making a move (good job someone was). And so, at the Christmas party, another actor made a comment about my dress and Chris remembered what he was planning to do: chat me up.

It was like a scene from Grange Hill,[6] but with post watershed language, lots of alcohol and bad Christmas music blaring in the background.

I walked past him, trying to avoid eye contact, no doubt. But he offered me a cigarette (oh, those were the days – nicotine minus the guilt. Banished from both our lives now).

He said, 'You look nice.'

I said, with a girly giggle, 'Hehehehe. So do you.'

He lit my cigarette. I looked behind me, saw all my workmates staring with their own ciggies dropping out of their mouths, and then ran straight over to them to proudly and excitedly announce that 'Chris Connel just gave me a cigarette and said I looked nice!'

We then, in our posh frocks, stood puffing on our ciggies while staring over at Chris in unison.

6 British TV drama set in a high school complete with terrifying teacher, a sausage and a hit record about saying no to drugs!

Fuck. It's actually going to happen.

Moments later, I found myself at the bar with my dream fella. He turned to me with a romantic look in his eye and said, 'Give us a kiss. Let's give these cunts something to talk about.'

And that was it. I fell hopelessly, madly and deeply in love.

Fast forward a year, and I was living with Chris and Sam in Newcastle. So I eventually got what I wanted and landed in a grown-up world. A ready-made family. The stuff of dreams.

But the thing is, as wonderful as it was having these amazing people in my newly wholesome life, I still hadn't tackled *me*.

I had forgot about the fact that my anxiety and mood swings existed long before any of the troublesome shenanigans began. And without real effort, it wasn't just going to disappear as I had hoped ...

The other thing I didn't appreciate was the fact that anxiety could wear many a mask, and it didn't just out itself as panic.

If I could change one thing about my life, it would be to go back in time and be a better stepmum to the lad that has, luckily, turned out to be the most wonderful human being I know. I am so immensely proud of him.

I am told I was a good influence on him. I am told all parents are full of regret, that nobody is perfect and we all want to go back and do things again. But it doesn't stop that nagging feeling.

Sam's mum had her own health issues, so Sam lived with Chris. But me, I was good and wise and healthy and ready to step in and save the world. I could provide a stable family life. I was ready to take on this grown up challenge!

Denial. It might have been what I had always wanted, but it didn't mean I was fully prepared and wise enough to actually do it.

Yes, I took Sam on outings. We would go to the beach and the cinema and play crazy golf. I would buy him cool clothes and enrol him onto new activities, like jiu-jitsu and climbing. I attended his school performances and snuck out of work early to make sure I could see a school judo demonstration mid-afternoon. And I taught him how to make chocolate chip muffins and spaghetti bolognaise.

But I was naïve to think that was all there was to parenting.

I struggled with the love and support bit. I loved him and I wanted to support him. But I just wasn't very good at it. The day-to-day stuff, that is. If he played up, I argued back like a child. And what happens if you do that? Watch any episode of *Supernanny* and she'll tell you. World War Bloody Three, that's what happens.

'Doctor, I'm worried about my heart. When I get angry with my stepson, I get palpitations.'

The doctor assured me that, as the palpitations only lasted a matter of seconds before disappearing, it was most likely stress that was causing them, as opposed to a heart problem.

'Doctor, I'm struggling with my mood swings. I am being really grumpy and getting angry at home with my family.'

Blood tests were done. My periods were heavy and my thyroxine levels were quite low. Time to take a thyroxine pill.

A lifelong ambition for me and Sam – scaling Vesuvius!

But I was still getting angry – with my stepson, with Chris. And it really wasn't a rational kind of angry – if indeed such a thing exists.

I would blow like Vesuvius. And the stuff I was spewing out was as ridiculous and irrational as Donald Trump's Twitter stream. Once, I even threw a packet of chocolate hobnobs at Chris in a rage. Luckily they hit his arm. That's tantamount to abuse. It still makes me shudder thinking about it. Imagine if he had done that to me?!

I took everything personally. Everything was an affront. I would get so wound up I would explode into a fit of rage, shouting nonsense and shaking with wild eyes and an unwelcome accompaniment of heart palpitations. This could be over something as insignificant as whether to watch *Coronation Street* or *Dr Who* on the telly.

I once blew up at Chris over the way he cooked halloumi.

'What the fuck have you done to my halloumi?!'

'I've fried it, like you do, and like they do in Pave.'[7]

'That's not how they do it in Pave. You've turned my entire block of halloumi into Quavers.'

'Have I fuck. This is how you do it.'

'No it's not! I'm not eating that. It's burnt fucking Quaver cheese!'

With that, Chris stormed out and I sat and cried. Then I called him and we both realised how ridiculous we'd been. Chris suggested we pick up a Greggs for lunch instead, seeing as how the frazzled halloumi was now in the bin.

Apparently, he never liked halloumi anyway.

When the rows were that ridiculous the atmosphere could often be saved by us calling each other stupid names, like "spunk trumpet" or "twat-faced bellend". The giggles would bring us back to normality.

But that wasn't always the case.

---

7 A trendy bar we used to go to.

Often I would get so wound up that I'd completely drain myself of energy. I'd end up spending with 30 minutes to one hour feeling as flat as a fart. I'd lie on my bed sobbing, my chest aching, with crazy thoughts going through my head like *Might as well kill myself. Who would even give a shit? What's the fucking point?*

I won't compare these fleeting thoughts to somebody who really is at crisis point, because it wasn't like that. And they were just thoughts, but I didn't take them literally. They were more like angry, childish thoughts with an "I'll show 'em" edge. And when it passed, I'd be right as rain (aside from the immense guilt I felt about bringing rage back into our family home again).

I never had any trouble apologising. When my head wasn't spinning I had the best of intentions and the ability to see where I had gone wrong. And it's good to say you're sorry. But how many more times can you say it? When does this behaviour become the norm?

Luckily, it doesn't happen anymore. Well – maybe it does still happen occasionally. But generally things have become easier – calmer – for reasons you'll see later in the book.

And Chris *never* offers to fry the halloumi anymore.

Our wedding day, with the best Best Man you could wish for (Sam was 12).

CHAPTER 8

Stereotype: The Professional Train Wreck

REALITY: FULL STEAM AHEAD!

117

Around the same time that I was blowing up like Vesuvius at home, I started panicking on public transport again ... and things were not going well in my professional life.

There are legal implications at play here, so I'm being suitably vague.

At some point during my career, in one of the three decades in which I have worked, I worked at some place in some industry in some region or other near where I lived. And it was there that I disclosed my anxiety to my colleagues and, as a result, had a seriously shitty time of it.

Having worked in PR for years, I am well aware that a good story needs a Who, What, When, Where and Why. And so I'm going to use a big metaphor while telling the story of the discrimination I faced in the workplace. Instead of talking about the workplace, I'm going to tell the story as though it was set in school. That way, I can protect myself legally.

So, let's set this story in school, in the 80s, somewhere in the UK ... and I'll add in a few nostalgic references just for fun. So, Spangles, Pacers and sugar are beer, prosecco and booze. School is work and the classroom is the office.

Former teachers, do not fret. I loved you, mainly. Some of you. This is just my way of making the story fictional.

So, I was in class and it was coming up to Christmastime.

'We're going to enter an important competition,' said the teacher.

'Oooohh,' said all the pupils in unison.

'We will be putting on a nativity play and competing against other schools across the country to put on the best show. Your headmaster is keen to see us reach the competition finals and place ourselves in the top ten of all the schools in England!'

The teacher looked serious. And a little scary. This competition was serious. This competition was scary.

'So,' continued the teacher. 'I need somebody who I can trust to run the nativity auditions, and bring together our school's best budding actors ... the finest talent we have.'

Oh god, oh god, don't pick me. Not for this. Not on my own. The headmaster has never given me a smelly strawberry scratch 'n' sniff sticker. I don't think he likes me as much as the others. Oh god ...

'Lucy!'

Noooooooo!!!

'I'd like you to take the lead on this, okay?'

'Of course, Miss. That's absolutely great, Miss. I'd love to, Miss.'

Some of the other pupils must have thought I was a creep. But I couldn't let anyone know I was scared of coordinating the nativity. It was important. And I'll be honest, it was quite a compliment to be asked.

Miss came to speak to me on my own.

'Lucy. This is a very important competition. If you get this wrong, we'll all be for it. Nobody will ever get a smelly sticker again. The class hamster will disappear. Breaktimes will be abolished! THEY WILL TAKE AWAY THE MILK. You must do a good job.'

Her tone of voice started to resemble that of my favourite angry American tennis player. ("You cannot be serious, man!" – I loved John McEnroe.) But it wasn't nice in real life. Or funny. It was abrupt. I couldn't break a smile into the conversation no matter how hard I tried. And our headmaster would never forgive me if I messed this up. I would never get my first scratch 'n' sniff sticker.

But this wasn't the only thing that was worrying me. The nativity was one thing. My messy brain was quite another. It was like having Mr Messy, Mr Rush, Mr Muddle and Mr Worry[8] all living in my head at the same time. I couldn't make any sense of my thoughts and worries.

8 These are all characters from the Mr Men children's book series.

I was having panic attacks and waking up at 4am every day, worrying about school. I was worrying about everything I had to do before Christmas and everything that could go wrong, about whether my classmates liked me. I was getting upset at home and upsetting my family at the same time. I was being shouty and angry and impatient. My head was getting fuzzy and it made it difficult to concentrate. And it wasn't just school either. I couldn't even enjoy my favourite programmes as much as I used to. All I could focus on in *Chorlton and the Wheelies* was Fenella the witch in the kettle who seemed more terrifying than ever before. *Trapdoor* made me jumpy. *Danger Mouse*[9] had my heart racing. It was like living my life every day in the opening credits of *Chocky*.[10] It was *terrifying*.

The things that I normally loved or enjoyed paled into insignificance, and the things I usually didn't let bother me were all of a sudden huge and impossible. I needed to channel Mr Brave, but the others weren't letting him in.

I had told Miss the week before that I had been having panic attacks and getting really frightened. I had taken a day off school and been to see my doctor. Because I had told Miss about this, I was hopeful she would give me some support. My classmates certainly did ...

'Miss, Kerry is going to help me with the nativity auditions. Is that okay?'

'No, Lucy. That is not okay. You can't have two people leading on this. It will become messy and confusing. You must do this on your own.'

I was so worried about the nativity competition that now even Madonna's Virgin Tour concert couldn't take my mind off it. I would usually skip home from school, massively excited to put the VHS video into the video player and recreate Madonna's dance routines with my best friend, wearing our homemade lacey gloves and cut-off tights

9 These were all kids' TV shows in the 80s.
10 A terrifying 80s children's drama based on the 1968 novel by John Wyndham.

and playing a tambourine. But now, all I wanted to do was sit in on my own. Instead of performing a carefully copied and choreographed routine to 'Material Girl', I just felt sick and stared into space.

My family started noticing something was up. I was eating too many sweets, overdosing on sugar. I thought Spangles and Pacers were the only things that would calm me down, but in reality, they gave me a bad head and made me feel faint. My mum would try to get me to eat something more nutritious.

'Here, Lucy, I've made you some crispy pancakes and Alphabites for tea. You must eat some proper food. You'll make yourself ill otherwise. You can have it on a tray while you watch TV.'

'I don't want them. I'm not hungry. I just want Spangles.'

I went into school feeling upset and shaky. At the end of the school day, just before the bell rang, I was called to a room with my teacher, a teacher from another class, and a couple of her pupils to talk about my progress with the play.

'Lucy. Where are you at with this?' Miss barked at me. 'I'm not confident that you're delivering on this project.'

I felt my face blush and my eyes water. I started feeling shaky. How embarrassing. Miss had just shouted at me in front of other pupils. They all sat there in silence.

'Err, I've written a plan of what needs to be done and when, and Kerry is helping with ...'

'I thought I told you Kerry was not to help you with this! Kerry has her own things she needs to do.'

'Err, okay ...'

'And another thing: your plan is not detailed enough. There's nothing there. We don't even know exactly what times the auditions are taking place.'

'But we do. I have planned stuff in ... see, look.' I was getting frustrated and knew my voice was starting to get loud and defensive.

Miss looked at the others and rolled her eyes.

'We will discuss this later!' she snapped.

I walked out of that room, got on the school bus, and cried. In front of everyone. I was so embarrassed. I ran home and sat in my room, sobbing uncontrollably, tears spilling onto my Victoria Plum duvet set, desperately trying to hide my face from the Corey Haim poster that was staring down at me from the wall. I felt so ashamed. I had been reduced to such a mess. A crybaby. A weak and pathetic crybaby.

'Miss was horrible to you,' one of the pupils said the next day. 'That was really horrid.'

The nativity coincided with the time that the school reports were coming out. They came out once a year. I had to meet with Miss on my own to discuss my report. I was nervous. I knew I had been very emotional and not myself. But at least I knew I had done all the things I needed to. Maybe I had just done them in a way that Miss didn't like.

'Lucy, your behaviour is having a destructive effect on your classmates.' She drew a big wiggly line with her biro. 'This is you.' She jabbed a finger at her wiggly biro line. Then she drew a less wiggly line. 'This, is what you should be. Do you understand?'

Yes, Miss.

Ugh. I felt awful. But maybe she was right. Maybe I was just being terrible in class. Maybe my work really was rubbish and messy.

'Are you scared of the headmaster? Is that what's bothering you?' she then asked, taking a much friendlier tone.

'Erm, he does make me feel a bit stupid. I feel more confident talking to the deputy head, but she's not working on this project.'

'Ha! Well! Don't trust the deputy. She'll just stab you in the back,' Miss snapped again.

Now I felt even more alone and stupid. Maybe the deputy didn't really like me either. Maybe she had said stuff about me to Miss.

I felt deflated, upset with myself, angry and guilty. Was my behaviour really that bad? I knew I had snapped a bit in the classroom, but that's because I had been so worried about the nativity and had been having panic attacks on the way to school most mornings.

In the end, Miss did put a classmate on the nativity project with me: a friend of mine. He took a look at everything that needed doing and advised Miss that the project needed more than two people on it. Yes, she said. She agreed!

How could she all of a sudden agree? She had said no to me when I'd suggested this! She had told me it was only enough work for one person. I was so wound up I could have burst out my uniform like David Banner in *The Incredible Hulk*. I felt like a cross between the Hulk and a Doozer[11] – raging inside, but small and helpless and unimportant.

I stood back. I let my friend do the work. I didn't want to become a pint-sized ugly green monster. The nativity passed without drama. We did okay, but we didn't make the top ten overall. Still, the headmaster didn't seem to mind. Funny, because I thought this competition was going to be as important as the inter-school sports annual competition.

The school broke up for Christmas and I tried to enjoy myself. It was my favourite time of year! It meant more Spangles and Pacers, spray-snow, foil ceiling decorations and the bumper edition of the *Radio Times*. It was great. I started having fun again. I was three full weeks away from the classroom. I felt relaxed and happy.

Then I had to go back.

'Happy New Year, Lucy. I hope you're calmer,' Miss said to me in front of the class. Great, my first ten minutes back in school and Miss had already referenced my moods before the break. I immediately felt anxious and wound up again.

11 A tiny, green character from the TV show *Fraggle Rock*.

And to make matters worse, I got my school report:

Lucy's enthusiasm to do her schoolwork well is obviously an asset. However, this enthusiasm, should she fail to keep it in check, could become her biggest hurdle. Her drive has led to some classmates suggesting that she can come across as self-absorbed. She is a very demonstrative person and she wears her heart on her sleeve. This can really energise the other pupils in class, but if her feelings are negative in nature, it can have a very destructive impact on those around her ...

At break time, I sat with my classmates and read them my report, feeling thoroughly deflated and upset. This was not going to go away.

My classmates said they knew I was struggling and that I could react badly at times, but they said I wasn't having a destructive impact on them. They said it was the teacher who was having a destructive impact on *everyone*. They agreed the teacher was bullying me. And they had been in my shoes before. They had reported the teacher before for the same thing.

Some of my classmates said they had seen Miss rolling her eyes behind my back, saying in front of the class that I was not managing things and blaming me for anything that went wrong.

It was time to discuss my report with Miss. I knew I had to confront her and say something. I'd read that this was the best thing to do before making a report to the school office. It was bloody nerve-wracking though.

'I feel like you're picking on me. It's really upsetting me. It's affecting my life at home.'

Miss laughed. She told me that I was picking on *her*. Everything I said she repeated back to me, as if I was the one who was doing it. We went around and around in circles.

This went on and on and on. The school office didn't really do anything. My classmates all stuck by me. They all told the school office. But nothing changed. Miss was good mates with the headmaster. Maybe that had something to do with it? Some of the staff left the school office and went to work elsewhere. One of them even told me they were frustrated at having no influence. None of this helped me though.

Fast forward to reality and my life as a real grownup. If that's what you can call it. I took some steps to solve my issues.

Number one – my doctor prescribed me with antidepressants and I got myself a therapist. With my brain seemingly producing the correct level of serotonin, I looked at what other life changes I could make.

Number two – the job. I got signed off work by my doctor. I had already started looking for something else. But I had this fear that any other job wasn't going to be as good as the one I'd just had. Weird, I know. Because it was hell.

Anyway, I somehow managed to impress at interview and land something new. God knows how, given that I turned up to the interview with a voice as ragged as Bruce Springsteen's and a seriously upset stomach, having been run down for some time. But I did it. In the words of The Boss, *'Wo – oh – oh I'm on fire!'*

I was signed off work until the new job started, so I was able to gather my thoughts and sort my head out without all that negative shite being drilled into it.

So I had a boost in confidence and I stayed off work, with weekly trips to see a therapist.

The first few days at home were really hard. I found myself waking up early every morning and shuffling around my house, doing my best impression of Max Branning (sorry – another soap reference. I obviously needed to get out more and stop indulging in *EastEnders*). I couldn't sit still, I had no idea what to do and I felt really guilty for being at home. Worse still, I stopped getting dressed and showering so much (it's funny, thinking back – becoming a writer means spending endless days in your pyjamas drinking endless cups of tea. I'm doing it right now as I type. I just happen to feel happier about it when I have a purpose and I'm not just sitting in my pyjamas and staring into space while my cup of tea goes cold).

I mentioned this to my therapist. She assured me that when you are off work with mental ill health, it shouldn't stop you from doing things that make you feel better. If I wanted to meet a friend for coffee, or go for a run, or enjoy a few days away or a shopping trip, then I absolutely should do it. I should listen to my body and do what makes me feel happy. And I should turn the guilt away like a club doorman turning away trainers.

Guilt – you're not coming in!

There is *no* arguing with a bouncer. Been there, done that, and obviously worn the wrong t-shirt. And footwear.

So I was not, under any circumstances, going to let guilt worm its way back in. I went for tea with a friend, mooched around the charity shops with my patient other half, and I went out jogging while listening to kick-ass tunes from The Prodigy and the Violent Femmes (I am now grown-up enough to accept that you can like more than one genre of music without losing your sense of identity).

So with a new perspective of the world thanks to my antidepressants, a lack of negative work vibes, supportive friends and family and time to take stock, things were on the up. Importantly for me, I became a better partner and a better parent. This was a true turning point in my life. And I am so bloody proud of myself for doing it and making those changes.

Because you see, this was me being strong. I wasn't being a weakling by running to the doctor. I wasn't a weakling for taking control of the situation and finding a new job. On the contrary, it was finding strength that allowed me to do those things – strength in myself and in my friends and family. I cannot stress enough how much it helps to have someone fighting your corner.

My family were amazing.

When the "madness" kicks in and you're about to fall off life's little raft again, it's a seriously lonely place to be. In fact, when you get to that point you're no longer paddling, you're fiercely bobbing under the waves, gasping for breath, and swallowing a shitload of toxic water.

I've never been shy about anxiety, but I have felt ashamed of it. When you're anxious, your mind confuses reality with fear – fear of what could become reality. You doubt your mind, your ability, your reality. And you start to wonder if the one thing you should fear is actually yourself.

Anxiety, especially when combined with real life problems, is more than a bitch. It's an evil, wailing banshee with Medusa's hairstyle and Cruella de Vil's painted talons scraping loudly down a blackboard.

The noise and commotion become so much that you can't separate your anxiety from real life. Until, that is, somebody pulls you back onto your life raft, points you away from the storm and gives you the chance to look at the horizon with a clearer perspective.

I've praised my family for being amazing. Well, so was a very good and loyal friend of mine. And I say that because he compromised himself by having my back when I was still at work.

I can forgive the amusing abuse I got from him. He was super posh (his hairstyle was reminiscent of Thatcher's 80s bouffant). He often insulted my latest charity shop bargain ('Which poor 90-year-old have you prized that monstrosity of a cardie from?') and provided a running critique about my hair ('What's with the Croydon facelift, darling? Did you wake up in 1992 today?'). But then, his designer socks and intense admiration of old-school celebrity cook Fanny Craddock were an easy target for me.

Fair's fair. Friendly banter.

But he was in no way fazed when he heard about my anxiety. And when he saw me struggling, he was there for me. He coached me through my troubles and demanded I join him in the John Lewis bistro after work for a prosecco (his choice, not mine – I'd have chosen a pint of beer at the Stand Comedy Club).

When it came to the crunch, when I needed someone to stand their ground and have my back about something that was actually happening and making my anxiety worse, he stepped up.

This was a good few years ago now. I remember thinking I was completely alone. But he changed that.

I cried my alcohol-soaked heart out to him one night. I felt mentally chaotic, completely hopeless, and totally ridiculous. I felt alone. Inside the home, I was kicking against the amazing support I had from my husband and stepson because I was so consumed with the stress I was experiencing outside the home.

But I *wasn't* alone. That night my friend told me that, without my knowledge, my husband, family and wonderful friend had been talking to each other a few days previously. Off the back of that, my friend stood up for me by speaking out at work.

It was such a relief to hear what was going on from someone else's point of view. I was hearing it from something other than my crazy, skewed, mashed up mind.

He backed up all of my concerns. He was in my corner. I wasn't fighting this fight alone.

I went home that night a different person. No, it hadn't immediately solved the problem. No, I wasn't suddenly in recovery. But I wasn't shouldering the burden alone. He was there for me. My husband and my mum noticed a huge difference in me. Something had lifted, and I went to work feeling stronger.

Regardless of his support, I still think my good friend has a ridiculous dress sense and an over bearing obsession with Hyacinth Bucket.[12] But we work well. And I will never forget his kindness. Even to this day, if I'm feeling a little angsty, he's there at my front door with a tin of home-baked fat rascals.

My only regret is that I ever doubted him. How could I ever think that such a good friend *wouldn't* fight my corner? If you can trust your friends with your drunken secrets and Breaking Bad DVD collection, then you can trust them with your mental health.

I just wish I could do the same for him. I still have no idea where I put his *Fear of Fanny* cookery DVD!

Bullying in the workplace is distressing. You think that it shouldn't be happening. Maybe it's *not* even happening, because you're a grownup. This kind of thing only happens in the playground, surely?

Nope. Not just the playground.

I know I set my story in a school, a fictional setting that sprang to mind because it was easy to link the bullying to such a setting. It made sense.

But adults are just as capable of bullying as children.

12 A comedy character from the UK TV show *Keeping Up Appearances*. Hyacinth likes to show herself off to others and pronounces her own last name as "Bouquet."

I know that there are always two sides to any story. And I know that there are often reasons for why things happen. Perhaps the bully feels threatened in other environments, or by other people. Perhaps they are super stressed.

I'm not going to get all angry about my story again. I don't know the full story myself. I only know what happened to me and the effect it had.

But one thing I do know is this: many organisations do not like to deal with this kind of thing. They try to shut it down as soon as they can, using any which way possible. So I wanted to share a few things I learnt through the process that might help other people. These points come from my personal experience and are not authoritative or expert. They're just a lay person's guide to navigating the scary employment law system (within my country, the UK – I can't say anything about other countries).

1. Human Resources are not independent mediators

As much as you would like to believe that the HR team are there just for you, you must remember that they are actually paid by the organisation you work for. And, if you're in dispute with that organisation, they have to have the organisation's back, or they risk losing their own jobs.

I'm not suggesting they are corrupt – not at all. I'm just saying that they might not have the power you assume they should have. Your HR Officer may well make recommendations to management. They may well know employment law and inform the senior team of what they are doing wrong. They may well empathise with you. But that doesn't necessarily mean that they can always stand up and shout on your behalf. We all have families to support and mortgages to pay.

Christ, I've worked in PR. I know I have fed the media lines that I didn't agree with. You have to toe the line. If you don't, you could well be putting your job at risk. It might not just be you leaving your soul at the door every time you walk into your place of work. It's a waste of time letting this fact upset you. Just be aware of it from the outset. Give them a chance, but don't assume it's a done deal.

2. Unions are not always fierce, left-wing fighting machines

Did you know that your union rep might *also* be employed by the organisation you're fighting against? That can and does happen. Conflict of interest? Apparently not. It's all above board. However, just like the HR Officer, union reps are real people with families and mortgages. So bear this in mind.

However, I still say you must sign up. You must give them a chance to help. After all, union members get free legal support. And if you have a mental health problem – and you're new to an organisation and therefore the culture that it breeds – then you absolutely should join up. Just to be safe. I've even known fans of Maggie Thatcher find solace and support from their union rep. You do not have to be in bed with Jeremy Corbyn.[13] You do not have to donate to the Labour party upon joining. I was quite happy to, of course (donate, not jump into bed with Jezza) but I know others who have been put off by it.

The only thing I will say, from my experience, is do your own research. You do not usually speak to the legal team directly; it usually goes through your rep. They are not actually employment law specialists. They may know more than you, but it's worth just checking with Consultant Google (see, sometimes it's a good thing) what you might be entitled to claim against.

3. Raise your complaint internally first

HR will probably advise you to exhaust the internal procedures first. And let me be clear, these internal procedures are about as pleasant as the internal procedures conducted by your gynaecologist. But as with the smear test, it is worth doing.

The thing is, if your complaint comes back as saying "no case to answer", that doesn't need to be the end of the process.

13 Current UK Labour leader. A real leftie!

You'll probably be led to believe that it is, that you've hit a brick wall. But that is simply not the case.

Not only do you need to be clear about what you have experienced, you also need to be clear about how these kinds of procedures should run. Go through the organisation's policies with a fine-tooth comb and check these against the advice of external organisations such as ACAS (Advisory Conciliation and Arbitration Service – they'll also give you some free advice). If your case has not been handled fairly, a tribunal will be just as interested in that as they are in the treatment that you have experienced.

4. You don't need Patty Hewes or Ally McBeal to win your case

Ooh we've all grown up watching those aggressive or glamorous US law programmes with lawyers tearing up the courtroom while wearing a slick Hugo Boss suit and killer Christian Louboutin heels. Well, I'm going to let you in on a secret. It's not real life. Similarly, you do not need to pay the expensive legal fees that pay for such workwear (especially when you're likely to rock up in Primarni).[14] Oh, and barristers can also be rather pricey, but that doesn't automatically mean they're better.

If you're not able to tap into your union legal team for representation, check in with Citizen's Advice. For me, it was a last resort, but I wish to God I had done it at the start. I was paying £200 per hour (I know!) but I didn't feel like I was getting anywhere. Citizen's Advice put me in touch with one of their employment specialists who runs an employment and discrimination advice and representation project. He charged a much more modest hourly rate. And not only was the hourly rate cheaper, but he worked quickly and seemed to soak up the information I gave him like a sponge. I didn't have to repeat myself over and over, therefore paying more fees to repeat work that we had already done. He wasn't abrupt or scary either.

14 A jokey term we Brits use to refer to clothing sold by a shop called Primark – combining Primark with Armani. Get it?!

Did that mean he would fail me? Absolutely not. In fact, his passion for justice was greater than his passion to simply look good and buy a new designer suit, which I think is more powerful anyway.

Another tip: roll up your Primarni sleeves and put the work in yourself – you pay less in the long run. I supplied my legal representative with a neatly ordered file, tons of detailed and dated conversations, medical reports, and copies of emails and text messages. It keeps the legal fees down if you do the admin.

5. Colleagues can do a U-turn on you

Don't forget that your supportive colleagues – who rallied around with cries of 'This is wrong! We will get you justice!' – may feel very differently when it comes to the crunch. Why? Again – families, mortgages. Don't waste your time getting angry or upset. You are not the most important thing in everyone else's life. They have mouths to feed. Just remember that if anyone does decide to stand up and speak on your behalf, they are making quite a sacrifice. I am forever indebted to someone who did this for me. It cost them too. But I think we can both confidently state that we are in much better situations today than we were back then. Silver linings.

6. Bullying itself isn't covered under the anti-discrimination laws, but it may be disability discrimination if it is related to, or because of, a mental health impairment

If your condition – over which you feel you have been bullied – has lasted longer than 12 months, and if it causes a significant impact on your day-to-day life, then you might actually be classed as disabled under the Equality Act. And if your illness is used against you in the workplace, you may well have been subject to discrimination. Check it out.

7. Weigh it up

Sometimes, just knowing that you did nothing wrong and that you can find another place to work is enough. Sometimes, it's worth more than the pain and stress you are likely to encounter by taking things further. Sometimes, taking things further could put you at risk of making your illness worse.

Weigh it up. Don't do what you think others expect you to do. Don't think that the most important thing is "getting them back" or "showing them". The most important thing is *you*, not them. Never forget that.

8. And finally ...

Do not let anyone make you think that you can't do it because you're weak or too "worried" about life. You're not. You have an illness. You're not weak. Always weigh up the pros and cons, but if you are adamant that you need to do this for yourself, then remember that you're no less likely to succeed because you have anxiety or any other mental illness. Don't let talk of expensive barristers or number of defence witnesses or baffling legal terms scare you. It's a tactic, not an advantage.

CHAPTER 9

Stereotype: The Happy-pill Popper

REALITY: THE GIRL IN RECOVERY MODE

So as I mentioned previously, this workplace stuff led me into my first experience of antidepressants. Well, other than necking one with a glass of Lambrini before seeing Tori Amos at Hull City Hall, that is. But given the amount of Lambrini I had, I don't recall any side effects.

There's one thing that I must make clear. Taking meds absolutely can be part of the holistic approach to therapy. They are not for everyone. They shouldn't be given out like sweeties. But they can be part of a wider approach, and you shouldn't be made to feel like a failure if you find value in them.

I'm neither a psychiatrist or a psychologist, but I'm a consumer of both ideas. So I reckon I can say something on the subject ...

The thing is, I sometimes follow what feels like a Twitter war: the Psychologists vs. Psychiatrists war of words in 140 characters.[15] It can be as caustic as JK Rowling vs. Donald Trump, except in this war, as far as I can tell, there isn't really a bad guy. And in this war, capital letters are only used for diagnoses and prescription pills.

As someone who pops antidepressants on a daily basis and pours her heart out to a complete stranger on a weekly basis, I find it all a little unsettling. Should there be one right way to do things? Am I in with the "in crowd"? (In taking antidepressants, I fear not.)

Still, they feel as though they work – for me at least. And the thing is, as much as long-term psychological treatment can unravel deep rooted causes for my anxiety, it's only available in six-session blocks on the NHS. Those six-session blocks can sometimes seem as much a sticking plaster as an antidepressant.

So you might need something to help you along in the meantime.

It took me a while to accept meds. I rejected them in the form of beta blockers and antidepressants for two decades before I decided I really needed to try something new.

15 Or 280 characters now, since it's been increased for everyone!

But I'm not an advocate for a one-stop chemical shop. Absolutely not. Even if you find that meds help with symptoms, it's good to use all the available tools – the cognitive behavioural techniques, the psychological, person-centred therapies – to address the problem too.

It might sound a little clichéd, channelling the inner child and all that shite, but something really has clicked for me of late. And it's because, after taking pills and going through CBT programmes, I have decided to look backwards, to delve into who I am and why anxiety might be a problem for me. All of a sudden I feel as though I have found the secret door to happiness. I just need to find the guts and strength to kick that bastard door to pieces. I've ignored it in the past, that door, and looked the other way. I pretended it didn't exist. I assumed it was far too heavy and thick to be moved. And even if I did sometimes confront it, I assumed there was a sheer drop behind it that would send me spiralling into a bottomless pit of hell, with Napalm Death's "music" ringing in my ears and a severe infestation of spiders, rats and Piers Morgan.

But all of a sudden, I am feeling a little giddy. That door feels more breakable. I reckon I just need Mr Miyagi[16] to teach me how to kick with confidence and belief. And I'm mega excited to find out what's behind it.

Liberation isn't a scary thing. It's an enticing thing – something that can take me into a world where I can read a script with passion, unafraid of sounding silly; where I can shout whatever I like as loud as I want at a basketball game; where I can sing along to Bonnie Tyler's 'Total Eclipse of the Ear Worm' on a karaoke machine; where I can jump into a pool and know I'm not going to die (the last of which is perhaps the most important to me).

So right now, I'm doing both. I'm embracing psychology and psychiatry. I absolutely see the value in both. And part of me believes

16 The mentor in the film *Karate Kid*.

that, without the help of psychiatric drugs, my mind wouldn't have been calm enough to embrace the psychology. No blood test or lobotomy is going to prove that though.

My experience of antidepressants

I am sharing this experience with a great big fat caveat: no two people are the same. We respond differently to different meds and different therapeutic techniques. But for what it's worth, here's all the crap that went through my mind before I took the plunge into the world of serotonin, which, by the way, is a chemical we release in our brains that has an impact on mood. It's a positive chemical that apparently can be drained through stress and illness. On the other hand, it can be boosted in vast amounts by illegal party pills and then rapidly depleted the day after to even lower levels. Medication, however, is designed to normalise the levels you have in your brain.

After years of feeling anxious and rejecting medication, I thought I would give it a go.

So hello, serotonin.

Serotonin has become a good mate of mine. We never used to be that close. I thought we were, but serotonin was one of those fair-weather friends. First hint of troubled water and she pissed right off.

So when we recently formed a meaningful friendship – as opposed to a one-night stand in a dodgy club where she whizzed around my brain, gave me an explosive sense of ecstasy then did a runner, taking every last bit of "happy" I owned – things began to change.

I have always been an anxious, short-tempered, neurotic being. But I never knew it might be due to some mysterious little things inside my head called neurotransmitters (the umbrella term for brain chemicals that include serotonin). I thought I was just a pain in the arse.

Turns out, I am a pain in the arse. But I feel much better about it now.

I was prescribed a reunion with serotonin in the form of Sertraline when I was going through a particularly stressful time. It got me through it. But it also showed me that I needed to re-wire years of negative thought patterns and routines. Because, with serotonin, I was happy and relaxed.

Of course, rewiring my thought patterns is a project I had to do in partnership with serotonin. She gives you peace and a better perspective on life, but if you want it to last, you have to put some effort in too. Give a man a fish ... etc., etc.

My experience of Sertraline was good. It's different for everyone, and I have heard that it just doesn't suit some people. In some instances, it can make symptoms worse. And in some instances, it can introduce new, negative symptoms. So I would never endorse it for others. But, for me, personally, it worked.

I was nervous, of course. I think that's perfectly normal. I remember a friend of mine taking it for the first time. He described the anticipation as "expecting the sky to turn red and crack open" when in fact he didn't really notice much. And neither did I (although I kept checking my pupils in the mirror just in case they'd blown!).

As I am sure many of us responsible adults of today can vouch for, a bunch of us misspent our weekends with synthetic serotonin boosters bought from dodgy types in nightclubs. Many of us succumbed to a chemical-fuelled rollercoaster ride at some point or other. And what do you get for it? A half-decent night that passes too quickly, dancing in a "higher state of consciousness" (no doubt looking like a possessed zombie on fast forward). You find a place you think you can only reach thanks to the severe serotonin assault on your brain (mind you, I can't think why anyone would choose to listen to Josh Wink sober).

Then you crash. And if you're anything like me – prone to anxiety, naturally short on serotonin – it's a really bad landing. There were so many Sundays lost to panic attacks, tears and *the fear*.

So, with a few bad memories from the 90s (and I'm obviously not talking about my Sun-In sprayed hair or high-waisted jeans) I collected my prescription and nervously swallowed my first antidepressant. And waited ...

Nothing.

I had a slight feeling of sickness for a couple of days, but nothing major to report. No buzz. No blown pupils. No panic. No weird behaviour. I did not sit in my office swivel chair rushing my tits off with an inane grin across my face.

No. Contrary to my initial concerns, people can't tell you're on them by looking at you.

Days passed. Weeks passed. Nothing.

But that's precisely it. Nothing happened. And that was good. Vesuvius did not erupt simply because someone forgot to put the rubbish out.

Don't get me wrong, I still shouted abuse at the TV screen when *Homeland* killed off ... sorry, no spoilers! And my other half still wound me up when he added to his fish tank collection in the garage and his dirty sock collection in the bathroom. But it wasn't anger. It was mild frustration. It was relative (well, except for my *Homeland* response. I'm still not over that).

Think about being on a plane and sitting by the window. You're coming in to land. You look down and see the tiny little cars moving around, people obviously going about their business. You're able to sit back and take things in. Observe. Think. Consider what you see, what might be happening, where people might be going and why.

On the flipside, imagine being in the centre of those cars, in the middle of a busy city. The noise, the pollution, the chaos.

To me, personally, that's how Sertraline feels. Sitting on the plane. Being able to step back. It inhibits the angry, panicked reactions borne of my overactive amygdala. I still see what's happening; I still consider if it makes me upset, happy, angry or irritated. But I take a moment to consider my response. And because I take that moment, other people respond better to me.

And that's the difference between Sertraline and the serotonin you unleash on the dance floor. I'm no scientific expert (disclaimer!) but from my *limited* understanding Sertraline – of the SSRI (Selective Serotonin Reuptake Inhibitors) family – allows serotonin to hang around in your brain without it all being sucked back up into the cells where it hides. And so you experience the positives that this brings. It is a steady, controlled experience.

I believe street drugs, such as those that contain MDMA, flood your brain with a huge overdose of serotonin in one go. Your brain allows you to feel wonderful for a very brief moment, before zapping it all back up and leaving you more depleted and miserable than when you started. Should have listened to Zammo,[17] kids!

So my Sertraline journey had real benefits. There was turbulence, however, when I circled at a higher altitude for a little bit – raising my levels as I waited for the storm in my life to pass – then dropped it again for a while.

It can be a little bumpy if I'm honest, dropping your Sertraline levels. You need to be prepared for that. You have to make sure it's not a crash landing. You do it bit by bit, step by step. A bungee jump over a concrete pub car park, with the risk of burst blood vessels, never did appeal to me. But a gentle parachute over lush New Zealand greenery – with the occasional flutter of anxiety – is much more manageable. As a natural worrier, I took this gentle approach to the extreme and split my pills into two, going from 100 mgs to 75 to 50, over the course of a month.

As my levels have gently decreased over time, I have felt flashes of anger or irritation on occasion. And I have heard others talk about "brain zaps" – strange head experiences that can occur when you

17 A heroin addict in the TV show *Grange Hill*. I loved that show.

come off the drugs. These can be a little unsettling, from what I can gather.

But this is precisely why you have to work in partnership with serotonin. You shouldn't rely solely on a chemical.

You need to keep working at that independent stuff you do even when you're in the midst of your relationship with a serotonin boost.

Psychotherapy. Training your brain. Rewiring your thoughts. It makes for a pretty effective life jacket.

So can I be fans of both please? Can we all go to the party together? I don't want to feel bad or think that synthetic drugs are my evil crutch. It's not my crack (that's Diet Coke if anyone's interested. Now *that* is an issue). Maybe one day I won't need to take the pills. Maybe one day I won't need to attend therapy. But for now, it's all good. And any negative feelings about taking meds will only set me back.

Although, contrary to my own previous beliefs, being set back does not necessarily mean heading back to square one on the mental health board game.

CHAPTER 10

Stereotype: The Relapse

REALITY: THE LAPSE

For me, the difference between a lapse and a relapse is how I perceive it. Believing I'm having a full-blown relapse at the first sign of trouble does me no favours at all. I've learnt that now. It's a self-imposed stereotype. The return of a few troublesome symptoms does not mean I'm a lost cause. It does not mean I have undone all my hard work and found myself all the way back at the start line.

In 2014, I experienced my first major, earth-shattering panic attack in over ten years. Want to peek inside it? Want to know what went through my head?

Warning – this experience describes detailed feelings of panic. If you think it may trigger your own feelings of anxiety, skip right over it. I won't be upset.

Return of the panic attack

I'm awake. It's 3am. My mouth is dry.

Why is it so dry? I stick my head under the tap. It's not working. I'm still thirsty. Too much wine? Salty food? Could be ... but this is extreme ...

More water, more thirst. This doesn't make sense. I feel uneasy. And it's so dark and still. I wish I was still. More water, more thirst ...

Red alert! Wide awake! There's something wrong. Some kind of rare reaction is taking over my body. I can't stop it. 3.17am. Has it only been 17 minutes?! Where is the daytime when you need it? Chris is sleeping. My fidgeting will wake him. I'll go downstairs, watch TV, take my mind off it. It has to be a panic attack. But in the middle of the night? Waking me from sleep? That's not right. And why now? It's been years...

Shall I go downstairs,   quietly? But then if I die, no one will know. There will be no chance of finding me in time. I'll be gone, and all I would have needed to do was wake Chris. One tiny thing that could save my life. More water first ...

Still not working. I'll have to wake Chris up. 'Sorry to wake you. I'm scared. I can't quench my thirst.'

'You're having a panic attack. It's happened before. It's okay. You'll be okay.'

3.23am. My god, it's creeping all over me now. Doom, pain, strangulation, death. Like ants crawling over my body, as fast as my thoughts.

I wrap my arms around my knees. Rocking. Quickly. My breath is fast. 'This isn't right. This isn't normal. Something is happening to me.'

'I promise you it's just a panic attack. Don't fight it. Let it happen. It will pass.'

'But it doesn't make sense. I keep drinking water. I can't quench my thirst.'

What if I've had too much? What if I've overcompensated? Nothing I can do now. 3.36am. Christ. How slow does the bloody clock want to tick? The faster my mind, the slower the clock. Where is the daylight?!

My breathing is bad. My heart is bad. My mouth is dry. I can't swallow. I'm going to die. It's definitely going to be tonight. This is definitely it. It's happening right now!

Chris talks to me. He won't indulge me. It's not comfort for my impending death. But why is he not panicking about having a dead body in his bed? And what about the life insurance – I never signed up. He's calm and kind, but logical. Rational. I slow to listen. He's talking me down and I think it's passing. Slow breaths.

'I think it's working.'

A prickling feeling runs up my chest. I'm up again. I'm going up again! Shit!

Focus. Calm. Slow down ...

It's 4.37am. It's finally happening. Daylight is coming and the clock starts ticking faster. I'm watching funny cat films on YouTube – he always knows best. One cat pushes another cat down the stairs and I watch it through and I giggle quietly. 5.12am. It's here ... like a rush of calm relief.

Morning is coming to save me.

I sleep.

7.30am. I wake. No emotions left. Just a flatness and a tiredness and a feeling of disappointment. Today is cancelled.

It was only when a counsellor explained to me the difference between a lapse and a relapse that I realised this panic attack wasn't quite the catastrophe I thought it was. A relapse might involve going back to previous behaviours and letting them take over. A lapse, on the other hand, is a setback. It might involve previous negative thoughts and behaviours, but it doesn't mean you've gone back to square one. If you don't let anxiety consume you, you can kick it into touch and pick up where you were when it rudely interrupted you.

So I decided to add the words of pop princess Britney Spears to my lapse – my blip.

I thought, *Oops. I did it again*.

Mind you, just because you accept it for what it is, doesn't mean the experience itself is sugary bubble gum pop. The experience can still feel frightening, but you have to remember that it's transient. It will fall out of fashion as quickly as 80s pop band Five Star did.

When anxiety starts following me around again, it takes on more of a Napalm Death-style, death metal persona. I can't bear Napalm Death. I can't bear anxiety lapses either. It's like I become that poor frightened soul who the "singer" of Napalm Death is screaming at.

That's probably the perfect way to describe it actually. For me, anyway. My anxiety attacks are like living with Napalm Death. Inescapable. Loud. Too much crazy shit running through my brain and screaming at me. And then, just when I think I'm reaching the other side, it crashes back from nowhere like a hidden track blaring out from a CD that I really, really hate.

The anxiety attack wasn't really my fault. I didn't "do it" to myself. Although I reckon not doing a few things kind of contributed to my brain having an almighty meltdown. It came to a head on 14th February.

Sadly, all my other half got for Valentine's Day 2017 was a headfuck.

He knew I was having a bad day, so he stayed home from work that evening. However, to cheer me up, he thought he'd treat me to a beautifully stunning orchid and my favourite alcohol-free beer (yeah, we're not rock 'n' roll. I think it's become apparent that I'd much rather chill with Cat Stevens than scream with Napalm Death.)

Sadly, when my lovely husband walked through the door with a great big grin on his face and gifts galore, his headfucked wife was pacing, shaking and crying hard. She looked like a member of Kiss who'd been caught out by heavy rain (note to self – buy the waterproof mascara next time).

He said he was going to be in at a certain time, and he wasn't. And I was worried about what had happened to him. I'm not going to describe the images I had in my head, in case they are triggering to some people. But they were bad. Really bad.

But here he was. Alive, well and offering me a beautiful orchid in a pot.

So the crash hit. And relief set in, but just for a moment. Because suddenly, from nowhere, I was up in the dark, stormy clouds with Napalm Death again.

I didn't get a second to rationalise my thoughts. There was like a chain of events happening in my head, going from nought to disaster – usually meaning death or worse than death. I didn't even have time to understand what that meant. It was just dark and dreadful. It churned my stomach and sent my arms into a furious prickling frenzy.

I went to the GP. I told him this wasn't right. I hadn't been this bad since my teens. I think I was hoping he might up my meds or give me some Valium or something. But he didn't. He began by infuriating me with talk of all those cognitive behavioural therapy tools I had learnt and not continued to put into practice.

This was not going to go the way I had hoped.

But then he said something interesting. He asked me, 'What would you do if you cut yourself? Would you sit there, watching yourself bleed, or would you grab a plaster?'

Hmm. He'd just compared my anxiety to a normal illness or occurrence. Of course I would grab a plaster.

So he told me I needed to grab a plaster. I needed to put those CBT tools back into practice, to stop the "crazy" stuff spilling out. I had to stop letting it happen, stop it getting worse and worse.

I always need to remember where the plasters are kept, he told me, and make sure they are accessible. It's no good sticking them in the loft to get dusty.

'It's like if you have a flood,' he said. 'You don't sit there waiting for the water levels to rise. You turn off the stopcock. But you will be much better at doing that if you know where the stopcock is in the first place. And you know that it works.'

'I've got a bit lazy,' I admitted to this GP, who was definitely more on the money than I had given him credit for.

I learnt all these tricks. I learnt how to rationalise my thoughts, drawing pie charts to understand the different possibilities that a symptom in my body might lead to. I saw on paper, in black and white, that there are hundreds of explanations as to why I might have a twitching thumb, and Motor Neurone Disease is actually one of the least likely, given a complete lack of other symptoms.

This was one of my tools in my CBT toolbox. And it had worked. But because I had then got better, I'd become complacent. I stopped putting my CBT into practice. And that's when it all started to come back.

Anyway, I finally managed to shut Napalm Death up. I stuck a great big fat plaster over the lead singer's mouth by rationalising my thoughts. I turned down the volume, and then I ejected that nasty little CD. I replaced it with Kylie Minogue, ate a Tunnock's caramel wafer, and cuddled a cat.

Screw you, Napalm Death.

The silver lining to having a lapse is knowing that I am not talking nonsense by blogging about mental health. I'm not faking ill. It's ridiculous, I know, getting imposter syndrome about something like that. Isn't imposter syndrome normally reserved for getting a new job and worrying you're not made of the right stuff? Or finding a new hair salon and thinking you're not worthy of being there because your nails aren't manicured and you don't wear lippy?

Who the hell panics that they are not ill enough, though? Me. I worried. I started to doubt my integrity ...

I don't have a real mental illness. I just worry a lot. I whine a lot. I'm as mentally ill as that vile Katie Hopkins is likeable. As the Daily Mail is tolerant. As Madonna is virginal.

As somebody who has often had health anxiety (not a real illness, so I have often told myself), it seems odd to try to make myself feel better by convincing myself that I *do* have a diagnosable illness.

The irony. It took all that CBT to stop me from looking for diagnoses for my 101 illnesses, and now there I was, worried that I *didn't* have an illness. And sometimes I still feel that way. I worry that all the other mental health bloggers with *real* illnesses will hate me for it. Self-stigma again – do I have Whiny Needy Twerp Syndrome, like Piers Morgan said of Will Young?

God, it's tiring. I might as well run a marathon with a fridge tied to my back.[18]

18 If you're not from the North East of England, google "Tony" and "Fridge".

I'm a Time to Change supporter, and yet I regularly beat myself blind with my own homemade form of prehistoric stigma. And the only way to remind myself that it's not all in my head? Getting ill again.

The reality is that even on 100mg Sertraline, I am not immune to panic. Drugs alone do not work. Increasing volumes of Diet Coke cancel out the drugs.

Slipping back into negative and indulgent patterns of thinking cancels out everything. And it still happens, on occasion, like on a recent Friday night. I had a dash to the toilet, followed by shaking, shivering, shallow breathing, tingling sensations in my arms, and a feeling of the chills in my legs and bum. It was real, all right.

Why does it always have to turn up out of the blue on a weekend? I had spent Friday lunchtime telling a good friend that everything in my world was bloody aces. I was looking forward to a night in. I went home happy. Then bam!

It must have been biting at my heels for a while. I must have got complacent.

I'm lucky to have a husband and a stepson who really get it. Well, I say lucky – it's actually been an unfortunate headfuck for all of us at times in our lives. But still, they get it and they don't say ridiculous things like "calm down".

My husband once led me in some breathing exercises. It worked. Until he started suggesting I hold the breath for longer. Like, for six seconds.

'I can't do it,' I said.

'Breathe properly,' he told me.

'I am! I can't do it for that long!'

'If you can't breathe in for six little seconds, you need to check in to A-&-bloody-E, because you're obviously suffering from some serious lung malfunction!'

I got massively impatient and irritable. Still, it wasn't panic-irritable. It was 'Chris, you're doing my head in' irritable. And that's kind of normal and reassuring in our house.

Not only did my panic subside, but my kitten climbed onto the bed and I fell asleep almost instantly, listening to her cute little purrs. Meanwhile, my husband turned on his MacBook to watch the latest instalment of *Ultimate Fighting Championships*. We work well together.

But I woke up the next morning with a familiar feeling of dread and that awful knot in my gut telling me that today was going to be dark and terrifying. Imagine watching *The Amityville Horror* on acid, with only Katie Hopkins and Donald Trump for company, while being forced to stick rusty needles in your eyes.

Chris talked to me again. It worked – again. Then I went for dinner and couldn't eat my pizza (anyone who knows me will know that something must be wrong if I can't eat my pizza). My stomach felt upset again, and I got hit with more strange chills and shakes and went to bed with another knot in my stomach.

Then I woke up. And it was gone.

I still worry about worrying. Has it really gone away? Will it come and bite me again?

I think about the triggers now. And rather than worrying about whether they are real cause for concern, I worry that I might panic upon encountering them. I worry that I'll summon the dread that is currently dormant within me, like when Gozer vanishes in the *Ghostbusters* movie only to be replaced by a gigantic Stay Puft marshmallow man. You can't relax knowing that a giant, marshmallowy cloud of anxiety could stamp all over your happy town of calm and suffocate you at any second. *Must. Stay. Alert.*

But maybe there's no need to stay alert, waiting for anxiety.

Calling on the help of supportive friends and family, kittens, Mr and Mrs card games, and Jon Ronson books helps me chase away the panic when I *know* it's returned.

I'm on meds. I know they're not 100% panic-proof (blatantly) but my lapse consisted of 36 tiny hours. And as my wonderful husband said, 'Don't run away from it. Face up to it, look it in the eye and tell it to do one!'

Anxiety, you're fired.

(For now anyway – it's a start).

I think, more than anything, the key is knowing that while I may always be prone to anxiety, I can handle it. I know how to handle it. I have the tools to handle it. And I have enough people around me – my family, my friends, my GP, my counsellor, my colleagues – who know enough about what it does to me to help me. They can say the right things. They can get me through my decreasing number of panic attacks. They can help me prevent panic attacks, because sometimes, just saying out loud to somebody that I am feeling on edge makes all the difference.

As some frozen princess once famously said – let it go.

And yep, the number of recurrences truly is decreasing. They're minimal. A blip. Meh!

Not that I am going to let myself get complacent again – that was a lesson learnt. I have Generalised Anxiety Disorder. It will probably pop up and say hello once in a while. But, just like the girls from the 90s Tampax adverts, I can still go rollerblading and swimming if I want to. (Not that I do – I think I'd rather watch a Sarah Millican stand-up comedy DVD with a pizza and a slab of chocolate, but each to their own.)

And if you want to hear something weird, here it is: there is always something good that comes out of the panicked experience. There's always a time that follows where you feel joyful. It's like breaking up and then making up. You've felt something so stressful; you've been wrapped up tight like a coil and now you've let all the tension go. And you're happily flopping down the stairs like a slinky toy that's in no hurry to reach the bottom. Because for once, you're living in the moment. And you're smiling, happy and relaxed. The kitten is purring, the ice in your drink is clinking, the candle is flickering and Sarah Millican's pants joke is making you laugh so hard that you nearly wet your own. But you don't give a fuck.

When you've been to Panic City, the joyful hygge nest is an amazing place to be. 1, 2, 3 – you're back in the room.

Self-help?

So what can you do when the lapse attacks?

We're all unique, so what works for me probably won't work for everyone else. But you don't have to sit cross-legged on a yoga mat while humming and practising mindfulness if you don't want to.

You *do not* have to buy an adult colouring book just because someone mentioned it in *Psychology Today* magazine.

I quite like colouring in, if I'm honest. And sketching. But just because people are making a business out of adult colouring books, doesn't mean it's the most effective form of mindfulness for everyone.

My mindfulness might involve heading out into the garden to put the world to rights with my ex-battery hens (I put that descriptor in so that you know that, regardless of the swearing, I'm a decent human being).

They love a good chatter. They're totally amazing to watch and I get fresh air while I'm doing it. I think perhaps the neighbours think I'm a little strange when I ask the feathered ladies if they had a good night's sleep and if they're enjoying their corn, but it works for me.

I guess the thing with mindfulness is that you can do whatever you want to do. Go for a walk to the beach. Relive your childhood by having a water fight. Go on a bike ride. Knit. Write. Play that new game where you have to wear an awkward mouthpiece and repeat complicated sentences without spitting all over your opponents.

Play *Just Dance* on the Nintendo Wii. Cuddle your cat. Re-enact the 80s dance routines to cheesy disco songs 'Superman' and 'Agadoo'. Stand in the shower and feel the water hitting your face. Walk on the grass barefoot. Watch ultimate fails on YouTube. Just be in the Right Now. It's pretty simple.

You *do not* have to pretend you like Yogalates. You don't have to sit and cringe in class when everyone starts chanting and all you want to do is laugh and fart.

We're all different. And I know often when I'm anxious I need to get rid of the "grrrrrrrrr" by pounding the streets in my trainers to a hardcore soundtrack. Sometimes I do enjoy the more chilled out versions of exercise, but we don't need to assume that it's the only way to get rid of anxiety. I've gone running before job interviews, when I'm angry, when I'm so tightly knotted I need to fight off the stilted adrenaline (mind you, go steady if your stomach's a bit knotted for other reasons – like the times I've had to make the dash to the loo after beer and curry night).

I blast those anxiety cobwebs off by running with The Prodigy blaring in my ears. For you, it might be Metallica. Or the Dead Kennedys. Or Destiny's Child. Whatever floats your boat. You'll feel the bloody power. You'll feel invincible. Oh, and if you want to make it through the working day feeling like a strong and powerful human being, then eat whatever your body tells you it needs. And really, who is going to judge you if you wrap a cheese and pickle sandwich in greaseproof paper, rather than shoving a load of edamame beans and beetroot into a Japanese bento box? That hipster at work giving you disapproving looks? Screw them! Deep down they might be craving a sausage roll.

There is no quick fix to curing anxiety, or indeed any other mental illness. And taking a walk doesn't magically fix it. But, as the supermarket ad says, every little helps.

You *do not* have to practise Feng Shui while wearing white linen pants and listening to Enya.

I like spiky plants. And I *will* have them in my house. I don't care what Feng Shui says. And heavily stocked bookcases. And patterned fabrics. Minimalist I am not. However, when my head is cluttered with mess, it doesn't help that my immediate and very real surroundings are as well (with the crap that's not meant to be there, that is). Sorting out the house can feel like a mean and impossible feat, like completing TV game show *Takeshi's Castle*.[19] You're never going to do it in a day ...

Wrong. You totally can. In a couple of hours. Especially with Kylie's bubble gum pop helping you out. Clear the decks, turn up the volume and throw your best shapes to 'Can't get you out of my head'.

You *do not* have to stand in front of your mirror, singing 'I'm simply the best' à la David Brent of *The Office* TV fame.

Because you'll look a right tit.

Basically, do what works for you. You don't have to be some kind

19 Has anyone *ever* won that game?

of hippy to practise self-help. And don't call it that if it makes you cringe. Call it Fuck You, Anxiety or Take That, You Piece of Shit, or ... *Expelliarmus!*

And what about those who don't suffer themselves, but love someone who does?

Things anxious minds do not want to hear

People (usually) are only trying to help when they suggest that you "calm down" or "just stop panicking". It must be hard to know what to do, I guess. Often people can swing between being dismissive and indulging the panic.

'Are you okay? Do you want to sit down? You look really unwell. I'm worried about you,' they might ask.

'Why? Do you think there really is something wrong with my heart?' is usually my response.

Loved ones must really think that they can't win sometimes. I'm lucky to have a husband who truly gets it, because he's lived it himself. But even then, in the midst of a panic attack, I can come across as awkward, irrational, and difficult no matter what he says.

For me, the best response is to be calm, pragmatic and supportive. That's not always easy if someone is hyperventilating in front of you, convinced they are going to die at any moment and complaining of heart irregularities. At what point do you call the ambulance? It takes a lot of getting used to the other person until you feel confident in knowing what to do.

So believe me when I say I do appreciate how hard it is to deal with someone like me (and that's not just in regard to panic – I'm told I am high maintenance and the most impossible person to make a satisfactory cup of tea for). However, to paint a picture of some of the worst things to say, I thought I'd outline a couple of things that really, really do not help.

"Don't panic."

Okay, I'll not panic. The end.

Are you kidding?! Do you think I would choose to be hyperventilating at 4 am if I had a magic panic on / off switch? And don't tell me to calm down. Don't make me angry. I'll turn green, burst out of my pyjamas then demand you drag me and my rapidly expiring body into A&E.

Tell me it's a panic attack. Tell me it will run its course. Acknowledge how terrifying it is. Remind me it can't kill me. Show me cute kitten videos on YouTube. Anything. Just …

DON'T TELL ME TO CALM DOWN!

"Stay strong."

Like I'm not! Don't get me wrong, mid-panic attack I'm not much use. But then if you're struck down with the Norovirus and your head's lolling over the loo, you're not much use either. Does that make you a weak person? I think not.

"You'll make yourself ill with worry."

You don't say! I've got 20-odd years' worth of medical records peppered with "patient appeared anxious", "patient offered beta blockers", "patient convinced her throat is closing up". Do you not think I am *already* ill?! I'm sorry I don't have a fracture or a luminous black and orange skin rash. But I will not request a lobotomy just to prove that an illness exists inside my head.

"You're not good with illness, are you?"

Erm. Yes, actually. When I know what I'm dealing with. My 17-year-old pneumonia-riddled pleuritic lungs did not stop me donning high heels and a 90s shift dress from Bay Trading Co, hitting the Blue Lamp pub and snogging my ill-suited, long-haired, over-friendly teenage boyfriend. Sadly.

As I have said before, it's the unknown I can't deal with, not the diagnosis.

"Have a drink."

Yeah, because delaying the inevitable, multiplying it by about a thousand, and letting it loose with the added complication of a blood sugar plummet and booze-induced amnesia is really going to help. A cup of Yorkshire's finest tea will do nicely, thank you very much.

Of course, I am so grateful for all the support I have received. But I guess it doesn't hurt to reiterate the "do nots". I'll not repeat them too much though – it could get as tiring as telling my husband my tea is too milky or he hasn't buttered my toasted teacake to the edges.

I said I wasn't weak – I *never* said I wasn't high maintenance.

CHAPTER 11

The Meerkat and the Spaniel

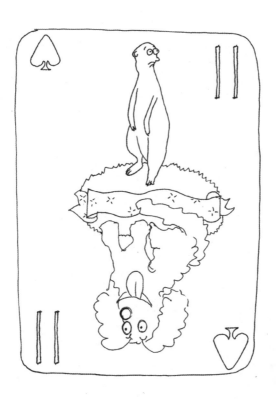

So this book is having a dig at labels and stereotypes. But sometimes they can be useful. If you can look at your anxiety demons or overexcitability in a different way, you can bring a little more light into your life. A counsellor and a good friend explained this one to me.

'Have you seen Meerkat Manor?'

I wasn't sure where my counsellor was going with this one. I had previously been asked to read various self-help books, but when she suggested I borrow her meerkat book I was slightly perplexed.

So she explained it to me. In meerkat communities there is always one "lookout" who is proactively looking for danger. They warn others of impending doom. That was me. I was that meerkat.

It's funny to think of your anxiety in animal form. You start to see it as a cute quirk rather than a terrifying element of your personality. A friend once gave me some advice about arachnophobia: 'If you see a giant spider, imagine it wearing a disco dress.' Cute, isn't it? (Although admittedly I still dance around like an uncoordinated Northern Soul fan when confronted with an eight-legged fiend!)

So did thinking of my anxiety as a meerkat make it stop? Of course not. But it did make me more accepting of it? Yes. And it helped me talk more openly about it, which has made a big difference.

My meerkat has been with me every day over the years, to varying degrees. When my husband leaves for work I hold him like it might be the last time. When the washer / dryer is on I complete a head count of the cats to make sure my lovely moggies aren't being drowned or burnt alive. Yes, the mental images are fairly graphic.

Some time ago, I waited outside M&S to meet my oldest girlfriends for hours of gossip and shopping, but my mind was elsewhere. I was busy googling "jaw cancer", trying (unsuccessfully) to reassure myself that I didn't have an aggressive tumour that was about to tear my face open. One side of my jaw felt slightly different to the other, and, after 48 hours prodding it, I was in a bit of pain. I have since had three separate professional opinions on it, all saying that it's just the shape of my face.

But the self-diagnosis changes every few weeks. I've had lymphoma, thrombosis, bowel cancer, heart defects and many more (including those two bouts of "meningitis" that landed me in A&E – both times being told 'You've bruised your skin by scratching it').

More recently, I've been obsessed with having a life-threatening allergy to hair dyes. When you're in your thirties with 50% greys, it's not a good thing to panic about. If you're going to hyperventilate on the number 38 bus, you want to look good doing it! And so my poor hairstylist has to spend an extra hour on my hair, using special products and foils so the dye doesn't touch my scalp. And why all the greys? She tells me it's probably stress related. I think she could be right …

I'm not belittling anxiety in any way. I've had panic attacks where I couldn't see or walk, or where I thought I was going to die. But it does help to think of it as my quirky trait, as nothing to be ashamed of.

Having accepted it, I decided to take control. Mindfulness, meditation, positive thinking, watching cute cat films on YouTube – these things do work! And, although it's not for everyone (and certainly not forever), medication is stopping the physical symptoms from making matters worse, giving me space to put the positive behaviours into practice. I am *starting* to understand it. And it is starting to understand that it can no longer propel me towards debilitating panic. At least not very often, anyway.

So I'm finally getting to grips with my rebellious little meerkat. Instead of fighting it, I'm learning to laugh with it. And maybe one day, I'll be *happy* to dance with the pretty little spider in her cute disco dress.

That's the story of my anxiety meerkat. So where does the spaniel come into it?

Simples! (as our friendly TV meerkats might say).[20] It's borne of my excitable nature – the good side to it.

My close friend Tom said to me early in our friendship, 'Lucy, you're like a spaniel. You're one full fat coke away from licking someone.'

I would never want to hurt my meerkat or my spaniel. And I am not sure that one could live without the other, so there's something to be said for accepting who you are. And the more you can do that, the less of a problem the dark parts of your illness will become.

---

20 If you're unsure what I'm referring to, check out the UK Compare the Market adverts. You won't be sorry.

CHAPTER 12

Where did it all begin?

So far none of the chapters actually tackle the beginning of my anxiety story. But I have only recently discovered it. My panic attacks didn't actually start with the pill and smoking and DVT and boyfriends. They started many years earlier. I just thought they were something else at the time.

You can rationalise your thoughts, manage symptoms with cognitive behavioural therapy techniques, cut back on caffeine, stop necking the Lambrini / chemical combos, grow up and get on with it. But if you dare to look back, there's every chance you might tackle the root cause of it all.

I have a new counsellor. I was referred because, during my counselling assessment, it was suggested that online CBT and management of symptoms probably wouldn't cut it. I'd done all that. It got me through but it didn't move me forward. It was time to tackle the big stuff.

Was I ready? As ready as I was when I ticked the option for GCSE Drama as an excruciatingly shy 15-year-old. As ready as I was when I jumped on the bus to travel to the Christchurch skydive centre.

So I very quickly said yes and committed before I could wimp out. After all, my amygdala might have told me I was bricking it, but my rational mind argued that these things would be bloody good for me. As good for me, in fact, as a Labour government would be for Britain. Anyway, back to therapy. Not that I would need so much of it if Labour got in …

Sorry, that's definitely the end of the political talk now. Back to therapy …

It's kind of interesting – having spent so many years managing symptoms and learning about CBT – to actually look at what's underneath, to look at what's driving it all. I had no idea until recently that a lack of self-esteem could cause anxiety, that it's not necessarily all the small things that make you anxious, but something much bigger and longer term that's driving it.

My counsellor pointed out that it was interesting how anxious I can get over the little things, and yet I smile and laugh about the big stuff – the stuff that made me who I am today.

Am I on a journey to find myself? Nope. Not like that. I'm not sitting cross-legged, ringing bells, and burning incense as I type. I'm just making sense of shit, that's all.

I've never felt that I was good enough. It's a dawning realisation, hence the new therapist. Something to do with approaching 40, perhaps? I've just always accepted that "good" isn't good enough. I've mentioned this before – remember when my husband suggested I take part in the Great North Run because I was starting to run a good distance? How did I respond?

'No, I can't compete in that. I wouldn't win.'

I need to learn to enjoy life, rather than feel compelled to live it. And to win at it. And to do it all *right now!*

So, my counselling sessions are going to help me look at which elements of my personality / illness I want to keep (which came first? Who the fuck knows?) and how much I need to let go.

Having a sense of urgency (no, not in the toilet sense – although that can happen when you're in your late thirties and go running a lot) can be both a help and a hindrance. Someone asks me to do something at work and it's pretty much done in an instant. I love a deadline. However, if that thing I was asked to do was, say, draft a press release to pitch out to editors, I need to know *right now* if said editors are interested. Tenacity is a great thing in PR – but when do I become a "tenacious" pain in the arse? Hmm …

So, balance is something I need. *Now!*

My brain is on high speed, my desk drawers are chaotic, my handbag is full of rubbish and no matter how many shelves or drawers I buy, there is never any free storage space in our house. And yet I create these little pockets of calmness around the house by, for example, arranging my wardrobe by colour or straightening up the sofa throws and cushions about three times a day. It's okay having acute little pockets of calm, but what I really need is a little bit of calm running throughout everything.

So my big lesson was to consider balance. What traits are good for me and useful, and what I could live more happily without? And to understand this, I needed to consider the five drivers. I hadn't heard of these before. They are:

Be perfect

Please others

Be strong

Try hard

Hurry up

I'm not sure which resonates with me the most – at the time of writing, I feel like they're all turned up to the max. But if I had to pick, then I'd pick the latter two. And I'll tell you something – it's really fucking exhausting keeping it up.

I've learnt that all of us have these drivers in our lives, to some degree. But we need to find a good balance. So I'll work through this in my counselling sessions – I guess I just need to remember that I don't have to conquer this anxiety thing yesterday, and I don't need to work overtime to accomplish it.

So I'll clock off now, have a cuppa and watch some shite on the telly. And I'll not be angry with myself if I wake up at 2am with kicky legs again. In fact, I'll make the most of it and just make another cuppa.

Right. I'm back. For another cuppa. Here's my childhood story.

I didn't have a traumatic childhood. But understanding something about who I am and the problems that created my social anxiety, awkwardness and worry has to be enlightening. If nothing else, it's a great big nostalgia trip back into the 80s, and we all love a bit of nostalgia, don't we?

So I'm going to take myself back even further in time. We all know memories are not 100% accurate, but I am going to *try* to transport myself back to the 80s when I first experienced panic, childhood fears, shyness and a massive amount of excitability ...

Forceps brought me into 1978. I arrived screaming loudly, starving hungry and wide awake. In fact, I never slept again for the rest of my childhood. At least that's how it felt for my poor mother.

I believe my mum was quite unwell after she had me. My sister followed just shy of two years later, narrowly missing out on being a 70s child (God – I feel old), and the complete opposite of me. She happily played alone, slept *a lot* (she even fell asleep on the village float while dressed as a 1920s Charleston girl) and was incredibly cute. Meanwhile, I never slept, constantly demanded attention, was always hungry and got my hair cut like a boy. It might have been

Distraught at being a Mr Man when my sister was a Little Miss.

Loving the excitement of the swings.

the direction that I, personally, gave the hairdresser in Tangles salon ('I hate my hair hanging in my eyes! Can you make it stop?') but I was so jealous when the older kids said 'Ahhh, how cute,' to my sister, and not a lot when they saw me.

While my little sister washed dolls' clothes and tottered about in Mum's high heels, I pretended to be tennis legend John McEnroe and played with Magic Sand.[21] Still, at least in the 80s we got chemistry sets, clackers and indoor fireworks thanks to our under-developed health and safety practices. They were fun.

And I loved all that fun stuff, but not My Little Ponies or dolls so much. Although I did discover a fun game with those lifelike baby dolls: lay them on the floor, take a running jump and stamp your Clark's shoes on them from a great height. The owner of the doll whose head flew the furthest was the winner. Not sure what a child psychologist would have thought of us kids decapitating baby dolls for entertainment, mind.

Still, even though I enjoyed playing with a bow and arrow and impersonating angry American tennis stars, I still dreamt of being Spiderwoman, not Spiderman. And She-Ra was definitely way cooler

21 One of the many 1980s toys that refused to live up to its reputation.

than He-Man. Girls could kick ass just as well. And so I never did get over the fact that my sister got to dress up as a Little Miss for playschool, and, for some reason, I had to be a Mr Man. That hurt. The tears that rolled down my face when my proud parents took that photo!

With me constantly expending vast amounts of energy fighting dark imagined forces – and racing boys on BMX bikes going "no-handed" down the hill – you might think I'd have been exhausted at the end of the day. But no. I was often in a heightened, excitable state that was so extreme I once threw up when I got my new bike for my birthday. Waiting for Santa became a stressful, nerve-wracking, night-long affair. And not just for me either – my poor parents must have grown tired of me shouting down from my bunk bed, 'Has he been yet? Has he been yet?!'

I was often up a height, which sometimes made me excitable. But it could also make me frightened too. I'd imagine the worst ...

Me, my dad and our gorgeous 70s sofa.

The things I was frightened of in the 1980s include:

Car washes

Wasps

Pylons

Other people

Beards

Volcanoes

I have recently come to realise that I have been anxious for most of my life, at least since I was a painfully shy toddler in junior Levi's (cool parents) and Clarks shoes (okay, *sporadically* cool parents). And, just like with my anxiety today, the things I was frightened of were never actually real.

I mean, of course a car wash is real. But I didn't *know* it was a car wash. I thought it was a big scary monster machine. A big, loud, whirring, growling machine that would move closer and closer until it completely surrounded our Scirocco, blacking out the sky with its menacing bristles that would reach out to grab me and pull me into the depths of hell. What if it broke through the windscreen? What if it took the roof off?

A merry 80s Christmas with my mum, sis and Shambles the cat.

It thump-thump-thumped on the roof of the car like villain repeatedly smacking someone over the head. The scary, bristly arms flopped down limply and all would be quiet again. But that wasn't the end of it ... A big, buzzing vacuum would appear from the sky and suck all the tiny water droplets on the windows to the front of the car. They'd move awkwardly as if trying to resist the force, until finally submitting and disappearing from view.

Silence.

My dad would turn the car ignition, Bruce Springsteen's ragged vocals blasting out of the tape deck once again. We'd roll out of the monster cage slowly and I'd breathe a sigh of relief. Or throw up. That often happened in cars too.

These things were scary to children, weren't they? I don't think I was unique. I just think that I carried these kinds of fears into my adult life. As a kid, you can't rationalise with yourself that a car wash isn't a monster. As an adult, you really should be able to. But I can't. I can't convince myself that a spot is not cancer, or a bruise is not meningitis. Monsters morph into many different things as you grow up.

I think my motives were different as a toddler though. Yes, I went on and on and on about minor injuries. A wasp (scary thing number two) stung my hand. I cried. And then, over several weeks, I intermittently pointed to the now non-existent wasp sting and cried again. And again. Sometimes I would even point to the wrong hand where said wasp sting never even existed. This usually coincided with a telling off. So rather than childhood hypochondria, I think this was more a bargaining tool to get out of trouble. My imaginary friend Toonit helped me in that respect as well.

'No, Mummy, I didn't do it. Toonit did it,' I'd say. Or, 'I know I hit my baby sister over the head with a steel tray, but that horrid wasp hurt my hand and made me cry. Please have pity.'

Children – master manipulators. All kids are total narcissists.

Another trait that has carried on into my adult life is my total inability to throw caution to the wind and have fun. I've definitely got worse since growing up. I begged and begged my dad to take me on the Alton Towers Corkscrew ride when I was little (we never did – apparently it was because I was too young). I won't even climb on the bloody Waltzers now, and the one-mile-per-hour Big Wheel makes my head spin. Going to the Hoppings fair with me is a dull affair. The log flume is as far as I'll go (that's just funny!) and I'll waste the rest of the time shooting at things that won't fall down or throwing hooks over ducks.

As an adult in my twenties, I remember jumping on a small flying fox (zip wire) in Raglan, New Zealand. As soon as I got on it and the speed began to pick up, my stomach moved sideways and my head spun. I spent the rest of the evening sitting in the shack, playing cards and drinking beer to get over it, while everyone else ran back up the hill for another go. The following day, seeing as we were in one of New Zealand's best surfing spots, we all trundled down to the beach for surf school. I sat on the sand. I felt so bloody jealous. Had I always been this boring?

As a kid, my dad would take me out to experience the more sedate ace kite flying. Which two-year-old wouldn't be ecstatic about their dad taking them over the railway bridge and onto the playing field to fly a brand new kite?

Me.

There were big, dark, scary towers with wires running across the sky (pylons – fear number three). My dad and his friend flew the kite, and I just sat somewhere nearby, staring suspiciously at the threatening electricity pylons. Shouldn't kite flying be a lovely, nostalgic memory? All I can remember is wanting to go home, put my pirate pyjamas on (see – gender neutrality was possible in the 80s) and remove myself from the inevitable and severe danger of kite flying in monster pylon territory.

Around this time there was a government "play safe" TV ad that didn't help. In it Billy sneaks through a gap in the fence to get his frisbee from the power station and ends up getting fried. Then the newsreader, through the radio, tells us he died. I bet that selfish girl who told him to do it has never forgiven herself!

That film didn't mess around. No bloody wonder I was frightened. It should have had an age 15 certificate!

But there were things that were even scarier than electricity pylons, wasps, or car washes: people. The sort that don't live in your house. That could have been anyone, really. Relatives, neighbours, the postman, the lollipop lady. I wasn't alone in this one. I carried it into my teens and my sister was just as bad as a child.

Aunt Sally didn't have painted cheeks or a husband with straw for hair – in fact, I think he had very little hair. And he wasn't called Worzel[22] either, he was called Frank.

Anyway, Sally and Frank lived in a nice house with a big 1970s fireplace and lots of brass stuff hanging off it. I liked it there, but it usually took me about an hour before I would say a single word. Getting a 'Hello, Aunt Sally' out of me and my little sister was like getting milk out of Margaret Thatcher.

It was the same wherever we went. We were like two little mute dolls in matching Marks and Spencer dresses, with big bows à la Princess Di, our best T-bar shoes and pretty white ankle socks with baby blue bows on them. (Our Junior Levis were not for best dress. I said our parents were sporadically cool, remember.)

When we were a little older, we went to see the *Sooty Show* with friends. Some lucky children were asked to go up onto the stage to meet Sooty, Sweep, and friends. It was us! They picked us! Well, in any other kids' eyes that would have been lucky. To me, it was

22 Explanation for the under 35s – Worzel Gummidge was a walking, talking scarecrow who appeared on the telly and whose unrequited love for cruel-hearted doll Aunt Sally did him no favours whatsoever.

like the most terrifying thing in the entire universe. In fact, it was about as terrifying as being trapped in a car wash with a swarm of wasps. The anxiety! I can't remember who went up instead but it was definitely one of our more outgoing friends, "normal" kids who no doubt skipped happily down the theatre aisle to the stage to meet the talking hand puppets.

'Outgoing' was not a word that could describe me as a child. I had so many little anxieties and I was shy in just about every situation. I was scared to use the toilet at school (for a number two), so, on more than one occasion I told the teacher I had a very poorly tummy, then my mum would pick me up to take me home. The relief when she picked me up was palpable (which was probably how she knew there was nothing really the matter with me). After three minutes in the downstairs loo I would be back to skipping around the house without a care in the world, asking to watch Look and Read with Wordy and begging to open a pack of ET biscuits. Anyone remember them? They were practically luminous green, orange and brown custard creams with a bizarre filling – possibly coca cola flavoured – wrapped in foil. No wonder I didn't sleep well as a child. The 1980s unapologetically pumped me full of E numbers.

Having my tea at other people's houses was often scary too. Not because my tea wasn't nice or the people weren't nice. My shyness would cause me huge problems when it was time to leave the table. My friend's mum made the best chips! Real chips – we still used fryers in the 80s. I can almost smell and taste them now. God, I loved dinners there. When the food was all gone it would be time to play with our flower fairy dolls (I had a Knight Rider car as well, okay). At my friend's house, when it was time to leave the table, we would have to say 'Please may I leave the table?'

Well, I couldn't do it. I absolutely could not do it. I have no idea why. I would sit happily chattering away about flower fairies (or Knight Rider) but as soon as I had to say that, the terrifying formal teatime phrase, my tummy turned to butterflies and my vocal range restricted itself to a barely audible mumble. Embarrassing or what?

It was the very same house where I fell from my friend's climbing frame after showing off doing roly-polies on the very top bar. It was one of those metal, triangular shaped ones with a swing in the middle that had a thin metal bar for a seat. I crash-landed with my legs either side of that bar. I ran home screaming. I remember a concerned and kindly old man knocking at the door to check on me and I hid in the lounge until my mum came home. I was so mortified that I had hurt my girl bits that I couldn't tell a soul – not even my mum – and I had to stifle the cries when I weed that night. Cystitis had nowt on that pain, I can tell you.

Anyway, back to the point.

My shyness got in the way of everything. My singing voice was also severely restricted. I am not sure if this was a blessing, given my recent rendition of Bonnie Tyler (Total Eclipse of the Earworm), or whether it was the shyness that stopped me from learning how to sing properly. Whatever it was, I was the only girl in my class who didn't make the school choir. Imagine that, aged just five years old! So when all the other angelic-voiced girls were singing 'Rise and shine and give God the glory, glory' in choir practice, I went to assembly with the boys to learn about the dangers of plastic bullets and acid rain. Yet more fear mongering. I was truly mortified being the only girl in assembly with the lads. And can I just point out, this was a state school. Inclusivity must have been forgotten during the drafting of that school policy.

'That girl can't sing a note. Throw her into assembly with the boys and let everyone know she's not good enough!'

Sounds more Dickens, doesn't it?

I'm not sure that anyone ever actually said that. But I know I wasn't allowed to go to choir, I know I was the only girl from my class in assembly and I know it was tortuous. Maybe that's why I have a memory of a McDonald's birthday party, me being the only girl at the boys' table while the pretty pink dress brigade ate their hamburgers and gloopy multi-coloured birthday cake at another table. I wasn't girly enough, because instead of sounding like Jem, the truly outrageous cartoon pop star, I had the weird, screwed up voice of *The Boy From Space*.[23]

What girl would have wanted to hang out with me, sounding like that? No wonder I had such low self-esteem.

Luckily, I had my friends from home – from the street I lived on – rather than from class. They were both girls and boys. I got to race cars with the boys and play with their Fisher Price toy garages and Tonka trucks. And I learnt tons from the girls – especially the ones who had big sisters. One friend, who was way more confident than me, introduced me to Madonna (bye bye, Bruce Springsteen. I'd rather get 'into the groove' rather than 'dance in the dark') and talked about boys. We wore jelly shoes and carried jelly handbags and wore suede slouch boots that smelt so good.

But being in the company of boys was another matter entirely. I played Kiss Chase at school, but only because I was desperate to hang out with the girls (and the one boy we all chased) and that was what they did. I remember the shame I felt when I was chatting to my friend from my street, the one with the fanny-splitting metal swing. I was sitting on the pavement as she hung out of her bedroom window, happily chatting about Madonna's outfits or whatever. The lad who lived two streets down – the lad who had an earring – came by. He was from a super cool family – his sister had at least eight earrings and his baby sister had two. Number of piercings was definitely a measure on the "cool" barometer. They also held garage discos where I didn't dance.

Anyway, we were maybe six or seven at the time, and, once earring boy arrived on the scene, my friend suggested, within earshot, that I might "love" him. Just like we loved Wham! and George Michael. Or A-ha and Morten Harket.

I immediately ran home.

23 Weird educational school's film from the 80s.

I had a similar reaction when I was running round and round the lounge 'dancing' to pop music with the little lad from down the road. It was boisterous and fun, but then he started singing 'my darling, my darling' (possibly singing along to some crappy 80s song about electricity and love and stuff) and so I said I wasn't playing any more. Any romantic notion was a step too far. And my face burned as brightly as Aunt Sally's (Worzel aunt, not aunt aunt).

In fact, any attention in that area continued to mortify me for years – right through to my teens.

I remember walking back home from PE one day in upper junior school, and one of the lads from my class started wolf-whistling at me. Well, I think it was aimed at me anyway. But I wasn't going to take any chances either way. I went into class the following day in my mum's shrunken woolly jumper with pastel pink and blue patterns around the neck, trying to look dorky and invisible. You might get away with it as a Christmas jumper these days, but back then it was pure cringe.

I rocked up to school in this itchy, woolly, pastel-coloured thing and my best friend was like, 'What on *Earth* are you wearing? You're usually trendy.' It was true. I was often the early adopter of fashions at that age – cycling shorts with luminous stripes down the side, ra-ra skirts, paint-splattered prints, tights cut off at the bottom to resemble Madonna's Virgin Tour days. However, I had an inkling that one of the boys fancied me and that was far too embarrassing. I would rather have adopted the Sunday school look and forget that I ever wanted to be a material girl.

A year or so later, when *Neighbours* was at the height of its popularity and we all started talking with upward inflections, I went to school donning my Kylie Minogue-inspired top, fresh from the teen range at Dorothy Perkins. It had no back, just braces, like the one Kylie wore in her *I Should Be So Lucky* video where she dances around her bedroom staring gooey-eyed at a photo of some unnamed Aussie hunk.

As soon as my cardigan came off, the entire population of boys in my class wolf whistled at me. And I don't remember the teacher making them stop. So I put my cardigan back on and sweltered in the July heat for the remainder of the school day. I never wore the top again.

Having more adult taste and knowledge than some of the boys was quite a hindrance too. I knew what a virgin was, because Madonna told me (well, Madonna sang it to me and my mum told me what it meant). So when the boys asked if I was a virgin, I said yes. Cue at least a week of them asking me who I had "done it" with. Still, they all shut up eventually. I can only assume they went home and asked their big brothers what it really meant.

So many possible mortifying slip-ups could happen at that age, such as calling your teacher "mum" by accident, watching a schools' programme featuring a character with the same first name as you, forgetting your PE kit and being told to play dodgeball in your vest and knickers.

'But Miss, I *am* poorly. Honest.'

'Well, you weren't poorly until you realised you forgot your PE kit, Lucy.'

No way would kids be forced to do PE in their underwear today. In fact, I think any teacher imposing that school rule would be swiftly arrested. Operation PE kit.

But things got much worse as I hit puberty – which I unfortunately did during junior school. I was absolutely traumatised that I got my period aged 11, on the night of the highly anticipated school disco. Doing the actions to the Superman song by Black Lace just wasn't the same anymore. As I "hitched a ride" and "combed my hair" and jumped up half-heartedly shouting 'Superman!' I was convinced that everyone in that dark disco hall knew I was hiding a terrible secret in my knickers. It's hard to get your head round it – you're growing up, but back to wearing a nappy. It wasn't until *Baywatch* hit our screens and I realised that actress Erika Eleniak couldn't be wearing huge padded towels in that barely-there swimsuit that I decided to take the plunge (literally) and switch to Tampax.

But with periods, at that age, you don't tell your friends (it's not cool until you're in high school and you've swapped your vest for a crop top or trainer bra) and so the only way you find out about who else has got theirs is by eavesdropping your mum's phone conversations to the neighbours.

'Oh, has Laura started too? Lucy did last week. She's definitely getting pubic hair too.'

Thanks, Mum. Thank god we didn't have a party line! Even so, we didn't have cordless phones in those days. So the thought of my little sister finding out about my traumatic puberty milestones, as my mum nattered on loudly in the hallway à la Sybil from legendary sitcom *Fawlty Towers*, made me cringe.

Still, it was comforting to know that the girl around the corner was in the same boat as me.

It wasn't just "down there" that bothered me either. Cast in the minor role of Fairy Lights in the school Christmas play, my silver leotard revealed two tiny bee sting boobies. If going on stage and speaking in front of an audience wasn't bad enough, letting the world know that my trainer bra days were fast approaching was sure to be crucifying. The only other girl in my class with boobs bigger than mine was lucky enough to be cast in the role of the Queen. So she was padded out with enormous fake boobs anyway. Nobody needed to know what was really there.

After saying my one line, I sat cross-legged on the floor at the front of the stage for the remainder of the play, firmly but shyly wrapping my arms around my chest. I had those Aunt Sally cheeks again!

Everything was embarrassing. Everything was cringey.

But people didn't just make me shy. No. Some people terrified me.

Scary thing number five. Beards.

Beards were seriously terrifying. Perhaps it was something about the unknown? I had no idea what was lurking behind those beards, with the exception of my teacher's beard. That didn't do a very good job of hiding anything, especially the fact that he had had peas and mashed potato for lunch.

When I was very young, my dad worked all hours building his own business. I remember my mum sometimes driving us out late at night, dressed in our pyjamas (probably my choo choo train pyjamas this time), to pick him up from the print factory. Sometimes we would go in. Some of his friends were funny and made us giggle. But there was one that had a beard. Now, this bearded man really scared me. I remember not being able to speak to him and wanting to hide from him.

My dad's beard had the opposite effect on my sister's beagle. Dad walked into the living room and Monty the beagle howled, growled and barked until his throat was hoarse. At least I didn't make a fuss. I just stared, peeking out from behind my mum's skirt.

Anything slightly different on a person could scare me. It wasn't just beards. The man with the hook, the man with the hearing aid, and the lady with the eyepatch all frightened me too.

One of my friends and I were outside playing near some flats one day when a lady with an eyepatch lent out of her ground floor window and offered us a Blue Ribband chocolate biscuit. Fear paled in comparison to our love of chocolate, so we accepted the Blue Ribband but didn't stick around to say thank you. We frantically legged it back to where my friend's dad was, frightened and out of breath. That lady was a witch (so said the anxious, prejudiced minds of two children of the 80s). After all, we were constantly told not to talk to strangers or bad things would happen.

Stranger danger was rife. In fact, as you may recall from an earlier chapter, a bunch of British kids were obviously so affected by this movement that when they grew up they became electronic band

The Prodigy and rallied other affected 70s and 80s kids all over the country. They created a swarm of colourful ravers moving repetitively to the childhood sound of Charley the cat. What did that song teach us again? Always tell your mummy before you go off somewhere.

Yep, the 70s government safety campaign soundtrack became a hit 1990s rave anthem. Perhaps government safety campaigns are to blame, for nurturing all this extreme childhood fear?

I also wouldn't speak to professionals. Especially doctors. I'm told I always left my mum feeling awkward when we went to see Dr Ball, whose rather large nose had me staring silently in disbelief. Was it real? Was he an alien? What was this facial protrusion? My mum would sometimes bribe me with a new board game from the shelves of the village post office, just to get me into the surgery for a measles jab or to get my earache checked out. Thinking back, I'm not sure what the point of attending the surgery was. No matter what was wrong with me, there only ever seemed to be two choices of medication. One was a bright red medicine that tasted horribly bitter. The other was a pink powdered formula that we mixed with water to resemble something close to strawberry milkshake. I quite liked that one until the girl sitting next to me in class puked strawberry milkshake all over my frilly ankle socks with the baby blue bow. I've never quite got over the pink milkshake / sick association. I stick to vanilla or chocolate these days. Painful memories.

All this terrifying stuff confronted me during the day, but at night my dreams were often haunted by the terror that the earth could inflict upon us all.

I loved sitting with my dad, poring over the pages of our big chunky world geography book. I was fascinated by natural disasters, volcanoes more than anything. I can literally remember every page on the subject in that book. I loved hearing about plate tectonics and magma and the earth's crust.

But once I fell asleep at bedtime, my little body laid peacefully on the top bunk bed with Flat Nose the teddy bear, my mind would take me into dangerous, volcanically active zones. The first one I remember appeared in my back garden in my dream, like a bonfire volcano. Another appeared in the middle of the cul-de-sac that I lived on. It was a complex array of bendy red and yellow pipes with a timer on it, like a spaghetti junction with lava. It was ready to blow! Another appeared as bubbling lava on the ground that I had to walk across to save my baby sister.

There weren't just scary monsters hiding in car washes and scary strangers with big noses and beards. For me, the very core of our reality was evil – and it could come and wipe us out at any given moment.

So at a very young age, as I played with Knight Rider cars and Magic Sand, I realised that life was full of uncertainty. Well, apart from the absolute certainty that my Buckaroo[24] game would break within a week of my mum replacing it with a new one. That kind of certainty was frustrating. Annoying, even.

But uncertainty was scary.

Uncertainty meant you had to make up your own ending to stories. And my endings were always wrapped up in danger and darkness.

But this is normal kids' stuff, isn't it? I mean, there are loads of us who survived the Great Thatcher Milk Robbery in the 80s (erm, a little British 80s politics there). And everyone had to transition from child to teen to adult. So what makes some of us more vulnerable than others? As I said, my childhood wasn't traumatic. My family wasn't rich, but we didn't want for anything (except a Mr Frosty machine I asked for every Christmas). I had a nice home life, a mum I could talk to about anything, and good grades at school (if you take my D in Geography out of the equation. But at least I now know that I don't live on a fault line).

---

24 A kids' game which involved placing heavier and heavier loads onto a small plastic mule, until at some unknown point it would jump up and throw off all the plastic equipment you'd heaped onto its back. Terrifying.

So, was it all my fear that lead to my adult anxiety? Nobody can prove that chemical imbalances have much to do with it (although I find some comfort in the idea of them). Perhaps, then, it was my personality. The personality and the genes I was born with, and how I soaked up the influences around me. I was a constantly excitable child, bursting with creativity. But I never felt good enough to share it. I was The Girl Who Just Wouldn't Speak Out.

Whatever people might believe, it is possible for children to experience extreme fears, anxieties and excitability.

May 1982

It's my birthday tomorrow. I'm getting a new bike from the bike shop. It's red and there is a ball of wool on it. And a basket. And stabilisers. I can't wait. It's coming tomorrow! Soon, I won't need stabilisers. Like that girl with the Raleigh apple bike across the road. I'm going to practise and practise and practise. I feel funny. I know they've got it in the house.

'Can I have it in my room? Why? But why?! I'm not going to bed unless you put it in my room. No! NO! But it's my birthdaaaaaay. But pleeeeeease!'

I love my bike. It's so pretty. I can't sleep.

'Muuuuum! Muuuuum! I feel sick! Muuuuum quick, it's coming. Muuuuuu— bleurghhhhhhhhhhh bleurghhhhhhhhhhh!'

It's got carrots in it again.

July 1987

'Mum. I feel sick. I dreamt about an oak tree. It was weird. I feel really sick. I'm frightened.'

I can't stop shaking. I don't like it. I feel really sick. I am not leaving the sink.

Okay, I wasn't sick. Where's Look-In magazine? I need to take my mind off it. I bet Madonna's not scared of throwing up.

I remember a mini-series of night-time anxiety that I experienced as a child. I thought it was about having a tummy upset. But I think that was perhaps the symptom. Let's look at it again in more detail.

I awoke in the middle of the night. Well, it felt like the middle of the night. It was probably 10pm or something. Regardless, my parents were tucked up in bed by this point.

I had dreamt about an oak tree. That was all I could see in my mind when I woke up. There's usually nothing scary about an oak tree. But this one felt dark and dreadful. It churned something up in my tummy and before I knew it I had woken my mum, telling her that I felt really, really sick.

My poor, patient mother then spent the next half hour with me while I hung my head over the bathroom sink and shook like a leaf. Well, it was more like a crazy fairground ride, to be honest. I wasn't sick, but I remember being terrified. And shaking. A lot.

The episode passed without me vomiting and I went back to bed. But this happened a few times. I was never actually sick, but I always woke up shaking, scared of being sick.

It was through one of my adult therapy sessions quite recently that I recalled these strange, nocturnal shaking fits. And it was then that I had a eureka moment. I have *always* been an anxious person. I have *always* had panic attacks. I just didn't know they were panic attacks.

It's quite fitting, really, that my first ever panic attack involved an oak tree. It reminds me of that folk tale, *Henny Penny*. (If this book has managed to reach anyone outside of the UK, you might know it as *Chicken Licken*.)

A cute little hen in a folk tale gets hit on the head by an acorn and rapidly jumps to the conclusion that the sky is falling in. After convincing a load of other impressionable animals that the world is coming to an end, she unwittingly reveals their vulnerable beliefs to a predator (a fox). The fox lures them into its lair for "safety" and then gobbles them all up!

Well, that's my interpretation of just one version of this age-old folk tale. And I guess this is one reason I grew up believing that anxiety made me weak – even if I didn't know the word back then. Basically, you were a "chicken" if you had an anxious mind and you needed to "man up" (men were believed to be stronger back then too).

(Some retellings of *Henny Penny* do have happy endings, though. The moral of those versions was not to believe everything you were ever told. It's kind of like an early version of cognitive behavioural therapy. Don't believe everything your mind is telling you. I would have done well to remember that, because my mind was about to start telling me I was going to die. Or worse still, piss my pants.)

October 1989

If I don't ask to leave class soon I will wet myself. I must wait until my teacher has finished reading out this page so that's there's a natural break and it's less embarrassing to ask to leave. Oh, Harper Lee – I love your writing, but why is this bloody chapter so long?

Can I feel it under my skirt? Have I already done it? Can I check without anyone seeing that I am checking for a wet patch? Oh god. I'm going to have to ask. What if I stand up and everyone sees and laughs and then I can't come back to school tomorrow?

On one. On two. On three.

'Miss, can I go to the loo, please?'

I'll walk sideways so no one can see my bum with the wet patch. Dash to the loo.

I'm here, thank god. No wet patch.

I don't need the loo after all.

The lesson I've learnt is that the panic attacks and anxiety didn't start when I was 15 years old. They started much earlier. For some reason, the way I processed the world around me and my own feelings and thoughts created problems for me as I grew up.

So, I had been there and worn the t-shirt (the mental health one, that is) long before I realised I had. It was an awkward fit, mainly because I never knew I was wearing it. I thought I was donning the "I'm Going to be Sick" T-shirt or the "I Can't Stop Shaking" sweater. That's what I was displaying to the world and that's how the world responded to me.

When you're a child, mental illness dresses itself as something else. And when you're a child of the 80s and 90s, like me, the idea of mental illness affecting you is entirely unimaginable.

But look back at my story. I mixed a shy and awkward personality that inhibited me in many ways, with the backdrop of the fear factors of the 1980s. Added in was perhaps a little too much adrenaline and too few hours' sleep because of it. From a very young age, I felt that I wasn't good enough.

Now, I am not asking you to break out the violins. I won't thank you for it. But not making the school choir might be the reason I refuse to take part in karaoke. Feeling overexcitable about getting a new bike might be caused by the same brain chemicals as my panic attacks. The clash between creativity and fear of expression no doubt caused inner tension.

I never felt that I fitted in. I never felt that I was worthy. I turn 40 this year. It's time to get the fuck over that shit.

THE FINAL CHAPTER

I am standard (a feel-good essay)

I've spent most of my life wondering why I wasn't up to "standard". You know, the average standards that your average girl aspired to meet. Of course, your average girl could never have actually reached those standards, mainly because they never truly existed.

But that doesn't stop us – it certainly never stopped me – aiming for whatever we interpret these standards to be. And when you're anxious and awkward, the path to them can be even steeper.

I have always felt like an outsider. I was so shy as a teen that I sat in the pub in utter silence (until I found what a bottle of Lambrini could do for my non-existent confidence).

And nothing I have ever achieved has been enough. I passed that PR course, but that other woman qualified at a higher level. I have a house, but theirs is bigger. I was shortlisted for an award, but I didn't win.

And what I am is a problem too. I'm a size 12 at Next, but a 14 at Top Shop. My legs demand that I buy short length jeans, not standard length. My hair doesn't fall and swish like the girl's in the Timotei ad. My eyebrows have thinned and my nails always break. But because they are so below standard, I don't feel comfortable even walking into a beauty salon to "fix" them.

Personality, anxiety, media. All of it plays a role in our confidence. And the pressure on our shoulders hits all of us in many different ways.

I started writing about my anxiety in April 2016. It kind of felt like when I point out my own giant zits to the rest of the office floor. If I tell the world how awkward I am, rather than the world telling me, I feel more confident, more in control.

And so I've said, 'Hello, world – my name's Lucy, and I have anxiety. Sometimes, I sit shaking on the bed, terrified I'm going to die. It's not pretty. But I can, and do, live with it.'

By October 2016, I was writing for *Standard Issue* – the magazine founded by comedian Sarah Millican. She was sick as a chip with all the bullshit she came across in women's magazines. There was far too much focus on how we looked and how flexible we could be when re-enacting something ridiculous from the *Karma Sutra*.

Just weeks later, I had a column. I was out to play a part in proving that we all meet the standard. I was joining Sarah Millican's fab feminist crew. Me! They actually let *me* into this choir of voices, all saying in unison 'I am who I am and if you don't like it, do one!'

I knew I wasn't alone when it came to mental illness. I had already joined Time to Change as an ambassador and had been open with many friends and acquaintances who lived with various mental health problems.

But with or without diagnosed mental illness, there are so many other pressures in life. They might trigger mental illness but, even if they don't, they're about as good for our health as Brexit is for the country.

Be skinny. Be beautiful. Be a sex goddess. Live like a bastard Stepford wife oozing perfection. Have manicured nails and a Hollywood smile. Keep on top of your Brazilian, take herbal hair remedies to make your mop shiny and never leave the house looking and behaving anything less than film star glamorous. In fact, don't even open your front door when you hit 35 – it's checkout time. (At least that's what the leader of the USA would have us believe. Female? Over 35? Useless!)

But then came *Standard Issue*. Sarah Millican told us she has IBS – she farts and she doesn't apologise for it. Not like that terrible episode of *Sex and the City* where Carrie's world comes crashing down around her because she let out a tiny excuse for a trump in front of Mr Big. FFS.

And then there were features with people like the gorgeous Taryn Brumfitt, a curvy body image campaigner who looks the bloody business. And she's happy about it, too. Sarah Millican talks about the famous Kate Moss quote in one of her stand-up routines.

Remember it? Tiny Ms Moss said 'Nothing tastes as good as skinny feels.' When Sarah M tore her to shreds, we laughed and felt like we were finally with the In Crowd.

Fucking hell. Something is changing.

A lot of us are no longer ashamed of nature. We celebrate it, loudly and proudly. And there are more of us than there are of the Stepford wives. In fact, they are extinct in reality and only exist on retouched magazine cover images or through carefully constructed personas lived out through social media.

But does saying 'I am standard' make me average? Absolutely not. I just meet new standards that I now understand are the real ones. Basically, to be real and human and fucking happy about it.

The *Standard Issue* movement (let's face it – it is a movement) and all the wonderful articles and conversations with contributors, editors and readers on social media made me realise that none of us are average. We all meet the standard. But we all do it in our own wonderful ways.

We all have unique potential and ambitions and aspirations. And that's okay. The *Standard Issue* community listens and supports that. It makes us roar with pee-inducing, wrinkle-inducing laughter along the way. And we like it.

I'm *all* woman – not just the bit the other magazines report on. And now I know that, I'm all the more delighted – and delightful – for it.

So what am I going to do with this new found confidence? Well, let's be honest, I'm not perfect at being imperfect. Not yet. I might never be. I still have 'fat' days. But I have more days now where I walk around in my pants and feel good about who I am.

In fact, when I think about the times my other half has felt immediately compelled to snog the face off me, it hasn't been when I've dressed up to the nines for a night out, freshly waxed with Bridget Jones pants concealed below a figure hugging dress. Nope, it more often happens when he sees me dancing around the kitchen in my pyjamas, singing along to Absolute Radio playing the Rolling Stones or Jesus Jones or EMF. My out-of-tune voice, along with my out-of-rhythm wiggling backside, reminds him how much he loves the shit out of me.

And that's when I remind myself how much I love life. And me.

There's no time for anxiety when I turn oven cleaning into a disco dance. Or when I sing my cat's song loudly and proudly (he has his own song to the tune of 'Cherish' by Madonna. That's okay, right?).

I'm not sitting here telling you that I'm cured. I will always have some anxiety within me. But I am on a really exciting journey that may well transform the levels of said anxiety and how I manage it. And this form of therapy is not about managing symptoms. It's not about restricting anything. It's about liberating myself. It's about loving myself.

I'm not there yet. I told my counsellor only recently that I found it hard to believe that I could, in fact, overcome this pitiful self-loathing, this inadequacy. My lack of confidence seems so much more difficult to overcome than managing the symptoms of panic. And yet, it's quite likely that if I could do it, there would be fewer anxiety symptoms to manage. Because as I now know, low self-esteem is likely to play a major role in my mental health struggles.

But now, I've come to believe that it's possible. That I have the potential to do it. In fact, I truly believe that I can.

And if I can believe that, maybe you can too?

ACKNOWLEDGEMENTS

With great big thanks to my ever-patient mum, sister and wonderful friends for putting up with me and my unpredictable swings between excitability and angst; to my fellow stigma-busting warriors, the Time to Change team and tireless campaigner Denise Welch, for all their mental health work and their continued support of mine. To *Standard Issue* for giving me a platform from which to holler and showing me that the in-crowd is, contrary to the high school belief system, inclusive. To my colleagues at Home Group, especially the mental health peer support group who are always there for each other, and to my lovely editor Stephanie, who carefully corrected my inaccurate hyphenation of "twat-faced bellend".

A special thanks to my amazing friend Tom for being in my corner when it mattered most, supplying me with homemade fat rascals and regularly offering acerbic critique of my dress sense.

For Jo, who has made this book come to life with her fabulously fun illustrations. You star!

And of course, my two rocks, the most wonderful husband and stepson a girl could ever wish for. Chris and Sam, I love you both to the starry moon and back xxx

the *Shaw* **mind**
FOUNDATION

Supporting children, adults and families
for better mental health. **#lets**do**stuff**

Sign up to our charity, The Shaw Mind Foundation
www.shawmindfoundation.org
and keep in touch with us; we would love to hear from you.

*We aim to bring to an end the suffering and despair caused
by mental health issues. Our goal is to make help and support
available for every single person in society, from all walks of life.
We will never stop offering hope. These are our promises.*

TRIGGER PRESS

Giving mental health a voice

www.trigger-press.com

Trigger Press is a publishing house devoted to opening conversations about mental health. We tell the stories of people who have suffered from mental illnesses and recovered, so that others may learn from them.

Adam Shaw is a worldwide mental health advocate and philanthropist. Now in recovery from mental health issues, he is committed to helping others suffering from debilitating mental health issues through the global charity he co-founded, The Shaw Mind Foundation. www.shawmindfoundation.org

Lauren Callaghan (CPsychol, PGDipClinPsych, PgCert, MA (hons), LLB (hons), BA), born and educated in New Zealand, is an innovative industry-leading psychologist based in London, United Kingdom. Lauren has worked with children and young people, and their families, in a number of clinical settings providing evidence based treatments for a range of illnesses, including anxiety and obsessional problems. She was a psychologist at the specialist national treatment centres for severe obsessional problems in the UK and is renowned as an expert in the field of mental health, recognised for diagnosing and successfully treating OCD and anxiety related illnesses in particular. In addition to appearing as a treating clinician in the critically acclaimed and BAFTA award-winning documentary *Bedlam*, Lauren is a frequent guest speaker on mental health conditions in the media and at academic conferences. Lauren also acts as a guest lecturer and honorary researcher at the Institute of Psychiatry Kings College, UCL.

Please visit the link below:

www.trigger-press.com

Join us and follow us...

@trigger_press
@Shaw_Mind

Search **The Shaw Mind Foundation** on Facebook
Search **Trigger Press** on Facebook